ISBN 978-1-330-56967-2
PIBN 10080023

This book is a reproduction of an important historical work. Forgotten Books uses state-of-the-art technology to digitally reconstruct the work, preserving the original format whilst repairing imperfections present in the aged copy. In rare cases, an imperfection in the original, such as a blemish or missing page, may be replicated in our edition. We do, however, repair the vast majority of imperfections successfully; any imperfections that remain are intentionally left to preserve the state of such historical works.

1 MONTH OF
FREE
READING

at

www.ForgottenBooks.com

By purchasing this book you are eligible for one month membership to ForgottenBooks.com, giving you unlimited access to our entire collection of over 700,000 titles via our web site and mobile apps.

To claim your free month visit:

www.forgottenbooks.com/free80023

Similar Books Are Available from
www.forgottenbooks.com

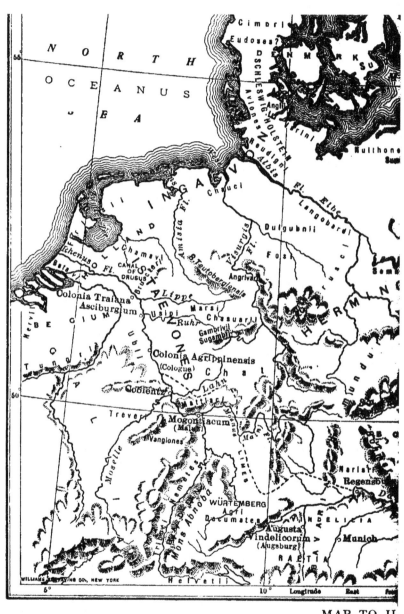

MAP TO IL

GERMANL

BALTIC SEA RUSSIA

SUEBICUM

Aes.

o Königsberg

Rugii

Lemovii

Gotones EAST

PRUSSIA

Oder

Halvecones

Vistula

Fl. Venedi

Nahanarvali

POLAND

Harii VANDILII OR

Viadua LYGII

SILESIA Manimi elisii

Marsigni

Riesen Gebirge

Fl.

Buri

GALICIA

Carpathian Mts.

Bastarnæ

MIA

Boii Cotini

comani MORAVIA

Quadi

Osi

AUSTRIA Vienna

NORICUM Aravisci HUNGARY Iazyges Theiss DACIA

PANNONIA Budapest

Greenwich 15° 20°

RATE THE

TACITUS

TACITUS
THE GERMANIA

WITH INTRODUCTION AND NOTES

BY

DUANE REED STUART

PROFESSOR OF CLASSICS IN PRINCETON
UNIVERSITY

New York

THE MACMILLAN COMPANY

1916

Norwood Press
J. S. Cushing Co. — Berwick & Smith Co.
Norwood, Mass., U.S.A.

PREFACE

In this country, as well as abroad, pedagogical tradition has long treated the *Agricola* and the *Germania* as coördinal elements of the Latin curriculum. This book, the preparation of which has been retarded by pressure of other work, is now offered as the companion of my edition of the *Agricola* (New York, 1909).

In so far as the intrinsic differences between the two treatises permit, the plan of this edition accords with that of its predecessor. The notes, necessarily somewhat more elaborate than the commentary on the *Agricola*, have been written primarily with an eye to the needs and interests of the learner. In conformity with a suggestion of the editor of the series, parallel citations drawn from works that are presumably known to the young student by name only, if at all, have been translated. In general, originality has been less a desideratum than reliability ; however, I have essayed to present my own summary and appraisal of the multifarious data which the last generation of criticism has yielded.

No editor of this book of Tacitus can claim the right to a hearing who has not taken strict account of the work of German scholars, who, conscious that for them, in a peculiar sense, the *Germania* speaks of

> " virum monumenta priorum,"

have made this field so largely their own and have delved in it *con amore.* I gratefully acknowledge my indebted-

DUANE REED S7

CONTENTS

INTRODUCTION TO THE GERMANIA

THE contents of the *Germania* were grouped by Tacitus under two main heads, the transition between which is indicated in chapter 27. The first of these divisions presents an exposition, general in character, of the geography of the country as a whole and of the universal features of the national civilization; the second part deals with the separate tribes and their distinctive traits and institutions.

In chapter 37 Tacitus gives a résumé of the collisions between Roman and German arms from the invasion of the Cimbri down to his own day. He sets as the chronological limits of this outline the consulship of Caecilius Metellus and Papirius Carbo, 113 B.C., and the second consulate of Trajan, 98 A.D. Evidently, then, the composition of the treatise falls in the latter year, which, it will be remembered, was marked also by the publication of the *Agricola*. The biographical tribute antedates the *Germania*, but the interval between the two works was at the most a matter of months only.

In the introductory chapters of all his other works, Tacitus takes his readers into his confidence and sets forth concretely the aims which have actuated him to treat his subject. In the case of the *Germania* alone, he departs from his practice elsewhere, and, with a directness truly Caesarian, plunges at once into his theme.

The fact that he was content that the title should speak for itself suggests that he regarded it as self-explanatory, as an adequate preface — unless we are willing to adopt, as an improbable alternative, the view that he chose to disguise his purpose and to force his readers to search for it between the lines.

The title — whatever the form in which Tacitus cast it — promises a geographical and ethnological treatise on Germany. A thoughtful perusal of the work cannot fail to convince one that the motive that controlled Tacitus in writing was simply that which the title indicates. He sought to acquaint his reading public with German lands and German peoples; the information which he proposes to impart forms his conscious end and aim. However, being Tacitus, he could not restrict himself to presenting an objective, encyclopedic body of facts. His personal bias and his subjective attitude toward his world frequently intrude themselves into the narrative. Tacitus was by nature too sincerely the censor as well as the mentor of his time and *milieu* wholly to repress his tendencies for long. His temperament could not brook divorce from his work.

Hence it is that many contexts of the *Germania* have a subjective coloring. This fact and the silence of Tacitus as to his object have given scope for speculation concerning the actual purpose of the treatise.

Some one has wittily said, "In Tacitus only Agricola and the Germans are good." This comment is as far from the truth as are most epigrams of the sort. Tacitus by no means depicts German life and character as flawless. Nevertheless, he eagerly embraces such opportunities as offer for contrasting the simple tastes and sturdy virtues of the Germans with the over-refinement and moral decadence rife among the upper strata of urban society in his time. Hence one trend of criticism has insisted on discerning in the spirit revealed in such contexts the design underlying the composition of the *Germania*. The treatise has been exalted into a sermon of ethical intent, uttered in arraignment of civilized man and his ways, in idealization of primitive, unsophisticated society

Tacitus has elements of the satirist and the moralist in his make-up. But it is not alone in the *Germania* that he breathes his conviction that "all's" not "right with the world." *O tempora, O mores* flowed easily from the end of his pen in all his work. Utterances or implications in this vein are invited in the *Germania*, more frequently than elsewhere, by the nature of the subject matter. However, to magnify them into an animus pervading the whole narrative and motivating it, is to do violence to the proportions of the contents and to regard as an isolated characteristic a point of view that is, to be sure, conspicuous in the *Germania*, but none the less a chronic feature of the author's temper.

Furthermore, comparison of the enlightened and the barbarous worlds was not a tendency original with and peculiar to Tacitus. Any civilization worthy of the name is prone to turn its eyes inward on itself and to estimate pragmatically its degree of success or failure. An integral part of this self-scrutiny must be inevitably comparative examination of other civilizations. The value of that which is local or present is measured most clearly by the foreign or the past. One result of the appraisal of itself undertaken by a culture may be self-satisfaction, as illustrated in the attitude assumed by the Greek toward the barbarian, the Jew toward the Gentile. Or there may come an opposite conclusion, carrying with it a sense of failure and the conviction that it is necessary to look to other peoples, other times, for life lived in a manner closer to perfection. Such a consciousness is given to asserting itself in a revolt against the complexities and the artificialities and the errors of the life of its own environment. Thus, a civilization spleens against itself and idealizes that which it is not.

In such contingencies men become *laudatores temporis acti* and plead the urgency of a return to the ways of the past. Sighs are heard from the poets for the renascence of the Golden Age. This Romanticism, as it is termed, was an outstanding tendency of the Rome of Augustus. It expressed itself in imperial policy; the fabric of the poetry of Vergil, Horace, and Tibullus is shot with strands of this hue. However, a malcontent civilization, pining to escape from itself, is not confined to focusing its gaze on the past. It may find exemplars of the ideal existence in circles of mankind contemporary with it but of a different environment. Thus, such an epoch discovers a devotion, more or less genuine, to an idyllic life in the fields and "under the greenwood tree." With Vergil it may exclaim, "*O fortunatos agricolas*" and body forth its penchant in pastoral poetry and "bucolic masquerading," as in the Alexandria of the Ptolemies, and the Paris of the later Louis. As a further variant of this enthusiasm, a movement back to nature may overstep the boundaries of nationality and find its admiration in foreign races untouched by the blight of civilization and still in the childhood of their development, where absence of desire is equal to riches and, in the words of Tacitus (*Germ.* 19), *plus . . . boni mores valent quam alibi bonae leges.*

The *Germania*, in so far as it reflects this spirit, is to be viewed merely as one expression of an attitude of mind which cannot be limited to a single writer or to a single age. Eulogy of the nature-peoples — if we may anglicize a convenient German compound — in its rudimentary form is as old as the Homeric poems with their references to the "blameless Ethiopians," dwelling in a remote quarter of the world, and to the nations of the far North, "milk-eaters, most just of men." The theme continued to be a favorite sentiment in Greek literature, prose and poetic. In Hellenistic times especially, when the strife and the unrest resident in social and political conditions impelled men to contemplate with approval and envy the lot of those who enjoyed a serene existence apart from the madding crowd, the topos developed into a formal mode of thought. Life according to nature was seriously advocated by the philosophers and its praises were sung by the poets. The historians did their part by extolling in ethnological descriptions the virtues of barbarous races and primitive epochs of civilization. In historiography the culmination of the tendency is represented by Posidonius of Apamea, a Stoic philosopher, a friend and teacher of Cicero. In an elaborate historical work, a continuation of Polybius, he set a mode in geographical digression and idealistic portraiture of peoples which exerted potent influence on subsequent exponents in kindred fields. In manner and in method the *Germania* is merely an exemplification of the type.

Knowledge of the literary antecedents of the *Germania* is important to us only as it contributes to an understanding of the mood in which the book was written. That phase of criticism which argued that Tacitus was governed by a definite satirical or ethical purpose, now belongs to the past. Another interpretation has had its partisans even in the present century. This school has professed to see in the *Germania* a kind of political brochure, composed primarily with the idea of shaping state policy in its relation to German affairs. Adherents of this view have formulated the author's motives in various ways : Rome was to be warned of the German peril, and the new emperor, Trajan, was to be moved to undertake vigorous offensive measures, or, *vice versa*, to be dissuaded from them ; the protracted sojourn at the German frontier on the part of Trajan, who had not as yet returned to the City since his elevation to the principate, was to be explained and justified. Any hypothesis of this sort necessitates the assumption that chapter 37 is the vital point of the treatise, and involves a deal of reading between the lines, a practice to which a writer who is so much a master of the subtleties of nuance and innuendo as Tacitus, easily tempts the critic. It is characteristic of the older interpreters both of the *Agricola* and the *Germania* to be caught in the pitfalls which the literary method of Tacitus prepares for them. Consensus of present criticism realizes that it is only by putting a fictitious value on isolated passages of comparatively slight extent and attaching a primary significance to passing allusions, that either work can be dignified into a piece of special pleading with political intent.

Nevertheless, the *Germania* stands in close relation to the events of its day. Rome's northern neighbors had been constantly obtruding themselves on her attention. Domitian's campaign against the Chatti (83–84) was still in the public memory; the great system of fortifications, which he had fathered, was being extended along the frontier and even, at certain points, pushed forward into Germany beyond previous lines of defense. The Quadi and the Marcomanni had sympathized with the Dacians in their outbreaks in 85–86. In the time of Nerva, Rome was threatened by a Suebian-Sarmatian *entente*. At the death of this ineffectual emperor, his energetic successor was at Cologne, where the problems of administration and organization of the German provinces were to claim his presence for a considerable period. In view of these facts the *Germania* may fairly be termed a timely publication. It is justifiable to infer that Tacitus, when he was writing the book, realized that it was bound to challenge attention.

Nevertheless, it would be an error to assume that the timeliness of the work and the fact that it dealt with matters especially germane to public interest, were the sole reasons which inspired Tacitus to treat the theme. The *Germania* stands in vital relation to the intellectual interests of its author. Therefore, we may be sure that he would have devoted attention to the subject in any case, at some time and in some form. We know that when the *Agricola* was being written, Tacitus had blocked out a work that afterwards took shape as the *Histories*. Ancient literary theory had long accorded a place in historiography to accounts of peoples and countries, even though such contexts were reckoned as digressions, hence were frequently introduced by some apologetic or explanatory formula. See, for illustration, *Histories* 5. 2. Many of the events which fall into the period covered by the *Histories* were staged in Germany, and German races were frequent participants in the action, as is evident even in the fraction of the work that has come down to us. The necessity of orientating and instructing the reader would have demanded the insertion of a modicum of geographical and ethnological material. Literary precedent sanctioned the incorporation of such data in a continuous context. That Tacitus followed formal practice in this respect, is shown by the presence of the digression on the Jews and their customs in the fifth book of the *Histories*. The stress which he laid on subject matter of the sort is conspicuously revealed in the *Agricola*, where he did not hesitate to transgress the canons of the biographical form in order to insert his account of the British peoples and country. In such a work as the *Histories* the extent of an excursus on Germany would necessarily be curtailed in comparison with the length of our treatise. Nevertheless, geography, ethnology, and political history would doubtless be represented, since all these elements are present in the similar digressions in the *Histories* and the *Agricola*.

In origin, therefore, and in kind, the *Germania* is a *by-product* of the historical studies of Tacitus. Whether he designed it to serve essentially as a substitute for an excursus in the *Histories*, dealing with the same data in briefer compass, it is unsafe dogmatically to assert. Under similar circumstances, a modern writer would be disposed to shape a treatise, covering one division of his field, into a complete preliminary to his greater work and thereafter to refer his readers to it by cross-reference and footnote. However, the devices of the literary technique of the present day cannot be posited without modification of the methods of ancient men of letters. In the time of Tacitus, treatment, in a separate essay, of a country and its inhabitants was not without precedent. Thus, Seneca, who, as a stylistic model, at least, exerted influence on Tacitus, had published books on Egypt and India. Hence the *Germania*, although it developed as a result of the literary interests of our author, was probably framed as a distinct work by him and not especially designed to hold a formal place in the sequence of his program of historical composition.

Our age prides itself on its devotion to scientific accuracy and to information gained at first-hand. No beauties of style would win a high place in our esteem for a book on Spanish America — let us say — which was not based on intimate personal knowledge of the countries and peoples described. The *Germania*, however, is the handiwork of the bookman and the stylist, and not of the traveler and the explorer. The treatise contains no convincing indication that Tacitus had ever visited Germany and studied the land and its inhabitants at short range. The literary ideals of his day would not have exacted such punctiliousness of him in amassing his material. Deference, of course, was paid to reliability, and artistic merits could not palliate falsification of data, either in the opinion of Tacitus or of his reading public. His own uncompromising attitude in this regard is expressed at the beginning of his account of Britain (*Agr.* 10) and is doubtless typical of the most severe criticism of the time. Here he claims highest respect for information based on authoritative observation by others, not on first-hand acquaintance. The same standards would hold good for the *Germania*.

According to the ancient criteria, of far greater moment in gaining the approbation of his readers than modern canons of taste would insist on in a work of corresponding content, were the presentation and manipulation of his material with a view to stylistic effectiveness. Although in the *Germania* Tacitus was handling a subject that would have lent itself to dry, encyclopedic treatment, the desire of esthetic appeal to his audience was as omnipresent as it was in the composition of the *Agricola*, notwithstanding the intrinsic difference in the themes of the two pieces. His favorite rhetorical devices and the stylistic mannerisms characteristic of this period of his writing are apparent throughout, from the typical locution in the first sentence, *mutuo metu aut montibus separatur,* to the poetic coloring of the idealization of the life of the wild Fenni in the last chapter. The conspicuous features of style and diction which are present in the *Agricola* are also discernible in the *Germania*.

It was not in consonance with the literary method of Tacitus frequently to refer by name to his authorities. Thus, in the *Germania* specific sources are disguised in such formulae as *memoriae proditur, accepimus, quidam opinantur, eorum opinionibus accedo.* Direct allusion is made to one author only, viz. Julius Caesar, who in chapter 28 is termed *summus auctorum.* In this passage as well as elsewhere in an instance or two, Tacitus reveals familiarity with the contents of the *Gallic War,* but in spite of his complimentary estimate of Caesar's credibility, Tacitus derived no data from him excepting the single quotation. Tacitus in numerous details stands at variance with his predecessor, and, as a whole, his picture of German civilization is far in advance of that presented by Caesar. Besides Caesar, a series of authors, Greek and Roman, had devoted more or less attention to Germany and the Germans before Tacitus essayed to treat the subject. Worthy of especial mention are Posidonius, Livy, who in book 104 discussed the geography of Germany and the customs of the people, the annalist Aufidius Bassus, an immediate successor to Livy and the author of a work cited as *Libri Belli Germanici*, Pliny the Elder, in whose multifarious literary achievements was included a complete history in twenty books of the wars which the Romans had waged with the Germans. Owing to the loss of these works and others which might conceivably have served him, and because of the absence of surface references in the *Germania*, it is impossible to fix the sources from which he derived particular data. We are reduced to speculation in which possible sources figure far more extensively than probable.

Dependence on the *Bella Germaniae* of Pliny may be assumed with great confidence. The title of this work as given by the younger Pliny, *Epist.* 3. 5, by no means justifies the conclusion that the contents comprised merely records of campaigns. That such a work might contain descriptions of races and institutions is demonstrated by Caesar's *Gallic War*. It is certain that Tacitus would have found in the *Bella Germaniae* ready to his hand a mass of the sort of material of which he stood in need. The elder Pliny had seen service in Germany and wrote as an eye-witness. He was a compiler of amazing industry, an observer who did not depend on memory to recall what he had seen but had notes taken on the spot. This' work of his was used by Tacitus in writing the *Annals;* see *Ann.* 1. 69.

Although, as has been said, the *Germania* was essentially the creation of a littérateur, it was not merely a compilation based on the work of authors of past generations. The occurrence in various passages of adverbial expressions such as *hodie* and *adhuc* (chap. 3), *nunc* (chaps. 33, 36, 37, 41), *mox limite acto* (chap. 29), *proximis temporibus* (chap. 37), and the like, shows that he took cognizance of events and conditions of his own day. He was informed as to recent shifts in tribal positions and changes of the frontier. His discussion of the tribes of the far north and of the eastern Germans bears, so far as our means of comparison extend, marks of greater originality and less dependence on literary sources than does his treatment of the peoples of southern and western Germany. Now, there was no lack of informants to whom he might apply for a knowledge of such contemporary affairs as had not been incorporated in books. Between the City and Germany there was a constant circulation of persons bound on military and official missions or engaged in mercantile pursuits. In the social stratum of Tacitus there were, of a certainty, many who had seen service along the Rhine and the Danube and had come into close touch with German life and affairs. The letters of his friend Pliny bear witness to the pains Tacitus took to secure data possessed by personal observers, when opportunity offered, in the composition of his purely historical works. We may be assured that the *Germania* contains the results of oral or epistolary inquiries directed to qualified informants, since this procedure is in accord with his literary method as we find it exemplified elsewhere.

In appreciating the *Germania* and estimating the value

of the facts which it presents, it is well to bear in mind that Tacitus, a Roman, wrote for Romans and not with an eye upon the demands of a later age. We must remember that he was intent, not merely on disseminating information, but on imparting to his work the most artistic form of which his talent was capable. In this latter object he has been eminently successful, even though the niceties of criticism force us to confess that the booklet does not reveal the fruition of his powers. However, we do not have to divest ourselves of modern literary ideals and adopt those of his own day to become sensible to the charm and the appeal of the *Germania.*

But it is something more than a work of literary art. Judged as an array of facts, it holds a position all its own. How far it would maintain preëminence in this respect, in case, by some impossible miracle, the works of all the other authors who dealt with the same theme should be restored to us, it is idle to speculate. Actually it stands as an indispensable repertorium for all who engage in the task of reconstructing the *Kultur* of our Germanic forefathers. It is, as it were, the golden *miliarium* about which center all the roads which the scientific excursionist into the domain of Anglo-German antiquity must tread. Modern scholarship would be thankful had Tacitus been more explicit on certain subjects, had indulged less in generalizations artfully phrased. It is tantalizing to suspect that rhetoric is sometimes invoked to cover a paucity of knowledge. Research in Germanic literary sources of later ages and the scientific application of linguistic evidence have thrown a flood of light on many obscure details. Since the nineteenth century the spade of the archaeologist has rendered yeoman service in uncovering the vestiges of Teutonic civilization from the Stone Age on. These discoveries have modified certain items found in the *Germania* and have largely supplemented it; but the accuracy of Tacitus has also been confirmed in an impressive fashion. In any case, the *Germania* has been and must remain a necessary adjunct to our apparatus of scholarship in its field. The testimony of the book and that of the remains interact.

It was a fortunate impulse which moved a leader in the intellectual life of his time, a gifted representative of the highest culture, to paint, while they lived in their land of forest, marsh, and mountain, those peoples who, in a few centuries, were to follow "the star of empire" to the south and the west, and, by destroying old worlds, were to make way for new. In modern Germany classical philologists and Germanic specialists have joined hands in the study of the *Germania*, with an enthusiasm sustained not alone by the spirit of scholarship, but by a patriotic fervor. Their pride in the possession of this monument of their antiquity and the intensity of their interest in it should be shared by the descendants of Angles and Normans in all lands and climes.

EDITIONS AND COMMENTARIES

Among the numerous textual and exegetical editions of the *Germania* may be mentioned:

R. G. Latham. London, 1851.

A. J. Church and W. J. Brodribb. London, 1869.

K. Müllenhoff. Berlin, 1873 (text).

A. Baumstark. Leipsic, 1876; revised 1881.

F. Kritz. 4th edition, Berlin, 1878.

A. Baumstark. *Ausführliche Erläuterung*, Leipsic, 1875 and 1880.

H. Furneaux. Oxford, 1894.

U. Zernial. 2d edition, Berlin, 1897.

C. Halm. 4th edition, Leipsic, 1883 (Teubner text, now in process of revision).

K. Müllenhoff. *Erläuterung. Deutsche Altertumskunde*, vol. 4, Berlin, 1900.

A. Gudeman. Boston, 1900.

E. Wolff. 2d edition, Leipsic, 1907.

H. Schweizer-Sidler. 7th edition revised by E. Schwyzer, Halle, 1912.

W. F. Allen. Revised by Katharine Allen and G. L. Hendrickson, Boston, 1913.

M. Hutton. Text and translation in the *Loeb Classical Library*, London and New York, 1914.

The following handbooks of recent date are convenient for reference on topics pertaining to Germanic history and antiquities

Fr. Köpp. *Die Römer in Deutschland*, 2d edition, Bielefeld and Leipsic, 1912.

K. Helm. *Altgermanische Religionsgeschichte*, vol. 1, Heidelberg, 1913.

Fr. Kauffmann. *Deutsche Altertumskunde*, erste Hälfte, Munich, 1913.

CORNELII TACITI DE ORIGINE ET SITU GERMANORUM

Germania omnis a Gallis Raetisque et Pannoniis Rheno 1 et Danuvio fluminibus, a Sarmatis Dacisque mutuo metu aut montibus separatur: cetera Oceanus ambit, latos sinus et insularum inmensa spatia complectens, nuper cognitis quibusdam gentibus ac regibus, quos bellum aperuit. 5 Rhenus, Raeticarum Alpium inaccesso ac praecipiti vertice ortus, modico flexu in occidentem versus septentrionali Oceano miscetur. Danuvius molli et clementer edito montis Abnobae iugo effusus pluris populos adit, donec in Ponticum mare sex meatibus erumpat: sep- 10 timum os paludibus hauritur.

Ipsos Germanos indigenas crediderim minimeque alia- 2 rum gentium adventibus et hospitiis mixtos, quia nec terra olim, sed classibus advehebantur qui mutare sedes quaerebant, et inmensus ultra utque sic dixerim adversus Oceanus raris ab orbe nostro navibus aditur. Quis porro, 5 praeter periculum horridi et ignoti maris, Asia aut Africa aut Italia relicta Germaniam peteret, informem terris, asperam caelo, tristem cultu adspectuque, nisi si patria sit?

Celebrant carminibus antiquis, quod unum apud illos memoriae et annalium genus est, Tuistonem deum terra 10 editum. Ei filium Mannum, originem gentis conditorem- que, Manno tris filios adsignant, e quorum nominibus proximi Oceano Ingaevones, medii Herminones, ceteri

B   1

Istaevones vocentur. Quidam, ut in licentia ᵛ
15 pluris deo ortos plurisque gentis appellatione:
Gambrivios Suebos Vandilios adfirmant, eaqu
antiqua nomina. Ceterum Germaniae vocabul
et nuper additum, quoniam qui primi Rhenum t
Gallos expulerint ac nunc Tungri, tunc Germ:
20 sint: ita nationis nomen, non gentis evaluisse
ut omnes primum a victore ob metum, mox e
ipsis, invento nomine Germani vocarentur.
3   Fuisse apud eos et Herculem memorant, p
omnium virorum fortium ituri in proelia canu
illis haec quoque carmina, quorum relatu, quem
vocant, accendunt animos futuraeque pugnae
5 ipso cantu augurantur. Terrent enim trepidan'
sonuit acies, nec tam vocis ille quam virtutis
videtur. Adfectatur praecipue asperitas soni e
murmur, obiectis ad os scutis, quo plenior et gɪ
repercussu intumescat. Ceterum et Ulixen qu
10 nantur longo illo et fabuloso errore in hunc
delatum adisse Germaniae terras, Asciburgium
in ripa Rheni situm hodieque incolitur, ab illo co
nominatumque; aram quin etiam Ulixi cor
adiecto Laërtae patris nomine, eodem loco olim
15 monumentaque et tumulos quosdam Graecis]
scriptos in confinio Germaniae Raetiaeque adhɪ
Quae neque confirmare argumentis neque refeller'
est: ex ingenio suo quisque demat vel addat fiⲥ
4   Ipse eorum opinionibus accedo, qui Germaniɛ
nullis aliis aliarum nationum conubiis infectos
et sinceram et tantum sui similem gentem exꜱ
bitrantur. Unde habitus quoque corporum, ta
5 tanto hominum numero, idem omnibus: truces

oculi, rutilae comae, magna corpora et tantum ad impetum valida: laboris atque operum non eadem patientia, minimeque sitim aestumque tolerare, frigora atque inediam caelo solove adsueverunt.

Terra etsi aliquanto specie differt, in universum tamen 5 aut silvis horrida aut paludibus foeda, umidior qua Gallias, ventosior qua Noricum ac Pannoniam adspicit; satis ferax, frugiferarum arborum inpatiens, pecorum fecunda, sed plerumque improcera. Ne armentis quidem suus 5 honor aut gloria frontis: numero gaudent, eaeque solae et gratissimae opes sunt. Argentum et aurum propitiine an irati di negaverint dubito. Nec tamen adfirmaverim nullam Germaniac venam argentum aurumve gignere: quis enim scrutatus est? Possessione et usu haud 10 perinde adficiuntur. Est videre apud illos argentea vasa, legatis et principibus eorum muneri data, non in alia vilitate quam quae humo finguntur; quamquam proximi ob usum commerciorum aurum et argentum in pretio habent formasque quasdam nostrae pecuniae adgnoscunt 15 atque eligunt. Interiores simplicius et antiquius permutatione mercium utuntur. Pecuniam probant veterem et diu notam, serratos bigatosque. Argentum quoque magis quam aurum sequuntur, nulla adfectione animi, sed quia numerus argenteorum facilior usui est promiscua 20 ac vilia mercantibus.

Ne ferrum quidem superest, sicut ex genere telorum 6 colligitur. Rari gladiis aut maioribus lanceis utuntur: hastas vel ipsorum vocabulo frameas gerunt angusto et brevi ferro, sed ita acri et ad usum habili, ut eodem telo, prout ratio poscit, vel comminus vel eminus pugnent. 5 Et eques quidem scnto frameaque contentus est; pedites et missilia spargunt, pluraque singuli, atque in inmensum

vibrant, nudi aut sagulo leves. Nulla cultus iactatio;
scuta tantum lectissimis coloribus distinguunt. Paucis
10 loricae, vix uni alterive cassis aut galea. Equi non forma,
non velocitate conspicui. Sed nec variare gyros in morem
nostrum docentur: in rectum aut uno flexu dextros agunt,
ita coniuncto orbe, ut nemo posterior sit. In universum
aestimanti plus penes peditem roboris; eoque mixti proe-
15 liantur, apta et congruente ad equestrem pugnam velocitate peditum, quos ex omni iuventute delectos ante aciem
locant. Definitur et numerus; centeni ex singulis pagis
sunt, idque ipsum inter suos vocantur, et quod primo
numerus fuit, iam nomen et honor est. Acies per cuneos
20 componitur. Cedere loco, dummodo rursus instes, con-
silii quam formidinis arbitrantur. Corpora suorum etiam
in dubiis proeliis referunt. Scutum reliquisse praecipuum
flagitium, nec aut sacris adesse aut concilium inire igno-
minioso fas; multique superstites bellorum infamiam
25 laqueo finierunt.

7　Reges ex nobilitate, duces ex virtute sumunt. Nec
regibus infinita aut libera potestas, et duces exemplo
potins quam imperio, si prompti, si conspicui, si antr
aciem agant, admiratione praesunt. Ceterum neque
5 animadvertere neque vincire, ne verberare quidem nisi
sacerdotibus permissum, non quasi in poenam nec ducis
iussu, sed velut deo imperante, quem adesse bellantibus
credunt. Effigiesque et signa quaedam detracta lucis
in proelium ferunt; quodque praecipuum fortitudinis
10 incitamentum est, non casus, nec fortuita conglobatio
turmam aut cuneum facit, sed familiae et propinquitates;
et in proximo pignora, unde feminarum ululatus audiri,
unde vagitus infantium. Hi cuique sanctissimi testes,
hi maximi laudatores. Ad matres, ad coniuges vulnera

ferunt; nec illae numerare aut exigere plagas pavent, 15
cibosque et hortamina pugnantibus gestant.

Memoriae proditur quasdam acies inclinatas iam et 8
labantes a feminis restitutas constantia precum et obiectu
pectorum et monstrata comminus captivitate, quam longe
inpatientius feminarum suarum nomine timent, adeo ut
efficacius obligentur animi civitatum, quibus inter obsides 5
puellae quoque nobiles imperantur. Inesse quin etiam
sanctum aliquid et providum putant, nec aut consilia
earum aspernantur aut responsa neglegunt. Vidimus sub
divo Vespasiano Veledam. diu apud plerosque numinis
loco habitam; sed et olim Albrunam et compluris alias 10
venerati sunt, non adulatione nec tamquam facerent
deas.

Deorum maxime Mercurium colunt, cui certis diebus 9
humanis quoque hostiis litare fas habent. Herculem et
Martem concessis animalibus placant. Pars Sueborum
et Isidi sacrificat: unde causa et origo peregrino sacro,
parum comperi, nisi quod signum ipsum in modum libur- 5
nae figuratum docet advectam religionem. Ceterum
nec cohibere parietibus deos neque in ullam humani oris
speciem adsimulare ex magnitudine caelestium arbitrantur: lucos ac nemora consecrant deorumque nominibus
appellant secretum illud, quod sola reverentia vident. 10

Auspicia sortesque ut qui maxime observant :• sortium 10
consuetudo simplex. Virgam frugiferae arbori decisam
in surculos amputant eosque notis quibusdam discretos
super candidam vestem temere ac fortuito spargunt.
Mox, si publice consultetur, sacerdos civitatis, sin privatim, 5
ipse pater familiae, precatus deos caelumque suspiciens
ter singulos tollit, sublatos secundum impressam ante
notam interpretatur. Si prohibuerunt, nulla de eadem

re in eundem diem consultatio; sin permissum, auspi-
10 ciorum adhuc fides exigitur. Et illud quidem etiam hic
notum, avium voces volatusque interrogare; proprium
gentis equorum quoque praesagia ac monitus experiri.
Publice aluntur isdem nemoribus ac lucis, candidi et
nullo mortali opere contacti; quos pressos sacro curru
15 sacerdos ac rex vel princeps civitatis comitantur hinnitus-
que ac fremitus observant. Nec ulli auspicio maior fides,
non solum apud plebem, sed apud proceres, apud sacerdotes; se enim ministros deorum, illos conscios putant.
Est et alia observatio auspiciorum, qua gravium bello-
20 rum eventus explorant. Eius gentis, cum qua bellum
est, captivum quoquo modo interceptum cum electo
popularium suorum, patriis quemque armis, committunt: victoria huius vel illins pro praeiudicio accipitur.

11 De minoribus rebus principes consultant; de maioribus omnes, ita tamen, ut ea quoque, quorum penes
plebem arbitrium est, apud principes pertractentur.
Coëunt, nisi quid fortuitum et subitum incidit, certis
5 diebus, cum aut incohatur luna aut impletur; nam agendis
rebus hoc auspicatissimum initium credunt. Nec dierum
numerum, ut nos, sed noctium computant. Sic constituunt, sic condicunt: nox ducere diem videtur. Illud ex
libertate vitium, quod non simul nec ut iussi conveniunt,
10 sed et alter et tertius dies cunctatione coëuntium absumitur.
Vt turbae placuit, considunt armati. Silentium per sacerdotes, quibus tum et coërcendi ius est, imperatur. Mox rex
vel princeps, prout aetas cuique, prout nobilitas, prout
decus bellorum, prout facundia est, audiuntur, auctoritate
15 suadendi magis quam iubendi potestate. Si displicuit sen-
tentia, fremitu aspernantur; sin placuit, frameas concutiunt. Honoratissimum adsensus genus est armis laudare.

Licet apud concilium accusare quoque et discrimen 12
capitis intendere. Distinctio poenarum ex delicto. Pro-
ditores et transfugas arboribus suspendunt, ignavos et
imbelles et corpore infames caeno ac palude, iniecta insuper crate, mergunt. Diversitas supplicii illuc respicit, 5
tamquam scelera ostendi oporteat, dum puniuntur, flagitia
abscondi. Sed et levioribus delictis pro modo poena:
equorum pecorumque numero convicti multantur. Pars
multae regi vel civitati, pars ipsi, qui vindicatur, vel
propinquis eius exsolvitur. Eliguntur in isdem conciliis 10
et principes, qui iura per pagos vicosque reddunt; centeni
singulis ex plebe comites consilium simul et auctoritas
adsunt.

Nihil autem neque publicae neque privatae rei nisi armati 13
agunt. Sed arma sumere non ante cuiquam moris, quam
civitas suffecturum probaverit. Tum in ipso concilio vel
principum aliquis vel pater vel propinqui scuto frameaque
iuvenem ornant: haec apud illos toga, hic primus iuventae 5
honos; ante hoc domus pars videntur, mox rei publicae.
Insignis nobilitas aut magna patrum merita principis
dignationem etiam adulescentulis adsignant: ceteris
robustioribus ac iam pridem probatis adgregantur, nec
rubor inter comites adspici. Gradus quin etiam ipse comi- 10
tatus habet, iudicio eius quem sectantur; magnaque et
comitum aemulatio, quibus primus apud principem suum
locus, et principum, cui plurimi et acerrimi comites. Haec
dignitas, hae vires, magno semper et electorum iuvenum
globo circumdari, in pace decus, in bello praesidium. Nec 15
solum in sua gente cuique, sed apud finitimas quoque civitates id nomen, ea gloria est, si numero ac virtute comitatus emineat; expetuntur enim legationibus et muneribus
ornantur et ipsa plerumque fama bella profligant.

14 Cum ventum in aciem, turpe principi virtute vin̄ turpe comitatui virtutem principis non adaequare. Iam vero infame in omnem vitam ac probrosum superstitem principi suo ex acie recessisse. Illum defendere, tueri, 5 sua quoque fortia facta gloriae eius adsignare praecipuum sacramentum est. Principes pro victoria pugnant, comites pro principe. Si civitas, in qua orti sunt, longa pace et otio torpeat, plerique nobilium adulescentium petunt ultro eas nationes, quae tum bellum aliquod gerunt, quia 10 et ingrata genti quies et facilius inter ancipitia clarescunt magnumque comitatum non nisi vi belloque tueare; exigunt enim principis sui liberalitate illum bellatorem equum, illam cruentam victricemque frameam. Nam epulae et quamquam incompti, largi tamen apparatus pro 15 stipendio cedunt. Materia munificentiae per bella et raptus. Nec arare terram aut exspectare annum tam facile persuaseris quam vocare bostem et vulnera mereri. Pigrum quin immo et iners videtur sudore adquirere quod possis sanguine parare.

15 Quotiens bella non ineunt, non multum venatibus, plus per otium transigunt, dediti somno ciboque, fortissimus quisque ac bellicosissimus nihil agens, delegata domus et penatium et agrorum cura feminis senibusque et in- 5 firmissimo cuique ex familia; ipsi hebent, mira diversitate naturae, cum idem homines sic ament inertiam et oderint quietem. Mos est civitatibus ultro ac viritim conferre principibus vel armentorum vel frugum, quod pro honore acceptum etiam necessitatibus subvenit. Gaudent prae- 10 cipue finitimarum gentium donis, quae non modo a singulis, sed et publice mittuntur, elccti equi, magna arma, phalerae torquesque; iam et pecuniam accipere docuimus.

Nullas Germanorum populis urbes habitari satis notum 16
est, ne pati quidem inter se iunctas sedes. Colunt discreti
ac diversi, ut fons, ut campus, ut nemus placuit. Vicos
locant non in nostrum morem conexis et cohaerentibus
aedificiis: suam quisque domum spatio circumdat, sive 5
adversus casus ignis remedium sive inscitia aedificandi.
Ne caementorum quidem apud illos aut tegularum usus:
materia ad omnia utuntur informi et citra speciem aut
delectationem. Quaedam loca diligentius inlinunt terra
ita pura ac splendente, ut picturam ac lineamenta colorum 10
imitetur. Solent et subterraneos specus aperire cosque
multo insuper fimo onerant, suffugium hiemis et receptaculum frugibus, quia rigorem frigorum eius modi loci
molliunt, et si quando hostis advenit, aperta populatur,
abdita autem et defossa aut ignorantur aut eo ipso fallunt, 15
quod quaerenda sunt.

Tegumen omnibus sagum fibula aut, si desit, spina 17
consertum: cetera intecti totos dies iuxta focum atque
ignem agunt. Locupletissimi veste distinguuntur, non
fluitante, sicut Sarmatae ac Parthi, sed stricta et singulos
artus exprimente. Gerunt et ferarum pelles, proximi 5
ripac neglegenter, ulteriores exquisitius, ut quibus nullus
per commercia cultus. Eligunt feras et detracta velamina
spargunt maculis pellibusque beluarum, quas exterior
Oceanus atque ignotum mare gignit. Nec alius feminis
quam viris habitus, nisi quod feminae saepius lineis 10
amictibus velantur eosque purpura variant, partemque
vestitus superioris in manicas non extendunt, nudae
brachia ac lacertos; sed et proxima pars pectoris patet.

Quamquam severa illic matrimonia, nec ullam morum 18
partem magis laudaveris. Nam prope soli barbarorum
singulis uxoribus contenti sunt, exceptis admodum paucis,

qui non libidine, sed ob nobilitatem plurimis nuptiis
5 ambiuntur. Dotem non uxor marito, sed uxori maritus
offert. Intersunt parentes et propinqui ac munera probant, munera non ad delicias muliebres quaesita nec quibus
nova nupta comatur, sed boves et frenatum equüm et
scutum cum framea gladioque. In haec munera uxor
10 accipitur, atque in vicem ipsa armorum aliquid viro adfert :
hoc maximum vinculum, haec arcana sacra, hos coniugales
deos arbitrantur. Ne se mulier extra virtutum cogitationes
extraque bellorum casus putet, ipsis incipientis matrimonii
auspiciis admonetur venire se laborum periculorumque
15 sociam, idem in pace, idem in proelio passuram ausuram-
que. Hoc iuncti boves, hoc paratus equus, hoc data
arma denuntiant. Sic vivendum, sic pereundum : accipere se, quae liberis inviolata ac digna reddat, quae nurus
accipiant, rursusque ad nepotes referantur.

19 Ergo saepta pudicitia agunt, nullis spectaculorum
inlecebris, nullis conviviorum inritationibus corruptae.
Litterarum secreta viri pariter ac feminae ignorant.
Paucissima in tam numerosa gente adulteria, quorum
5 poena praesens et maritis permissa : abscisis crinibus
nudatam coram propinquis expellit domo maritus ac
per omnem vicum verbere agit ; publicatae enim pudicitiae
nulla venia : non forma, non aetate, non opibus maritum
invenerit. Nemo enim illic vitia ridet, nec corrumpere
10 et corrumpi saeculum vocatur. Melius quidem adhuc
eae civitates, in quibus tantum virgines nubunt et cum
spe votoque uxoris semel transigitur. Sic unum accipiunt
maritum quo modo unum corpus unamque vitam, ne
ulla cogitatio ultra, ne longior cupiditas, ne tamquam
15 maritum, sed tamquam matrimonium ament. Numerum
liberorum finire aut quemquam ex adgnatis necare flagi-

tium habetur, plusque ibi boni mores valent quam alibi
bonae leges.

In omni domo nudi ac sordidi in hos artus, in haec 20
corpora, quae miramur, excrescunt. Sua quemque mater
uberibus alit, nec ancillis ac nutricibus delegantur. Dominum ac servum nullis educationis deliciis dignoscas:
inter eadem pecora, in eadem humo degunt, donec aetas 5
separet ingenuos, virtus adgnoscat. Sera iuvenum
venus, coque inexhausta pubertas. Nec virgines festinantur; eadem iuventa, similis proceritas: pares validaeque
miscentur, ac robora parentum liberi referunt. Sororum
filiis idem apud avunculum qui ad patrem honor. Quidam 10
sanctiorem artioremque hunc nexum sanguinis arbitrantur
et in accipiendis obsidibus magis exigunt, tamquam et
animum firmius et domum latius teneant. Heredes
tamen successoresque sui cuique liberi, et nullum testamentum. Si liberi non sunt, proximus gradus in posses- 15
sione fratres, patrui, avunculi. Quanto plus propin-
quorum, quanto maior adfinium numerus, tanto gratiosior
senectus; nec ulla orbitatis pretia.

Suscipere tam inimicitias seu patris seu propinqui 21
quam amicitias necesse est; nec implacabiles durant:
luitur enim etiam homicidium certo armentorum ac
pecorum numero recipitque satisfactionem universa domus,
utiliter in publicum, quia periculosiores sunt inimicitiae 5
iuxta libertatem.

Convictibus et hospitiis non alia gens effusius indulget.
Quemcumque mortalium arcere tecto nefas habetur;
pro fortuna quisque apparatis epulis excipit. Cum defecere, qui modo hospes fuerat, monstrator hospitii et 10
comes; proximam · domum non invitati adeunt. Nec
interest: pari humanitate accipiuntur. Notum ignotum-

que quantum ad ius hospitis nemo discernit. Abeunti,
si quid poposcerit, concedere moris; et poscendi in vicem
15 eadem facilitas. Gaudent muneribus, sed nec data imputant nec acceptis obligantur: victus inter hospites
comis.

22 Statim e somno, quem plerumque in diem extrahunt,
lavantur, saepius calida, ut apud quos plurimum hiems
occupat. Lauti cibum capiunt: separatae singulis sedes
et sua cuique mensa. Tum ad negotia nec minus saepe
5 ad convivia procedunt armati. Diem noctemque continuare potando nulli probrum. Crebrae, ut inter vinolentos,
rixae raro conviciis, saepius caede et vulneribus transiguntur., Sed et de reconciliandis in vicem inimicis et iun-
gendis adfinitatibus et adsciscendis principibus, de pace
10 denique ac bello plerumque in conviviis consultant, tamquam nullo magis tempore aut ad simplices cogitationes
pateat animus aut ad magnas incalescat. Gens non astuta
nec callida aperit adhuc secreta pectoris licentia ioci;
ergo detecta et nuda omnium mens. Postera die retrac-
15 tatur, et salva utriusque temporis ratio est: deliberant,
dum fingere nesciunt, constituunt, dum errare non possunt.

23 Fotui umor ex hordeo aut frumento, in quandam
similitudinem vini corruptus: proximi ripae et vinum
mercantur. Cibi simplices, agrestia poma, recens fera aut
lac concretum: sine apparatu, sine blandimentis expellunt
5 famem. Adversus sitim non eadem temperantia. Si
indulseris ebrietati suggerendo quantum concupiscunt,
haud minus facile vitiis quam armis vincentur.

24 Genus spectaculorum unum atque in omni coetu idem.
Nudi iuvenes, quibus id ludicrum est, inter gladios se
atque infestas frameas saltu iaciunt. Exercitatio artem
paravit, ars decorem, non in quaestum tamen aut mer-

cedem : quamvis audacis lasciviae pretium est voluptas 5
spectantium. Aleam, quod mirere, sobrii inter seria
exercent, tanta lucrandi perdendive temeritate, ut, cum
omnia defecerunt, extremo ac novissimo iactu de libertate
ac de corpore contendant. Victus voluntariam servitutem
adit : quamvis iuvenior, quamvis robustior adligari se ac 10
venire patitur. Ea est in re prava pervicacia; ipsi fidem
vocant. Servos condicionis huius per commercia tradunt,
ut se quoque pudore victoriae exsolvant.

Ceteris servis non in nostrum morem, descriptis per 25
familiam ministeriis, utuntur : suam quisque sedem, suos
penates regit. Frumenti modum dominus aut pecoris
aut vestis ut colono iniungit, et servus hactenus paret :
cetera domus officia uxor ac liberi exsequuntur. Ver- 5
berare servum ac vinculis et opere coërcere rarum : oc-
cidere solent, non disciplina et severitate, sed impetu et ira,
ut inimicum, nisi quod impune est. Liberti non multum
supra servos sunt, raro aliquod momentum in domo,
numquam in civitate, exceptis dumtaxat iis gentibus 10
quae regnantur. Ibi enim et super ingenuos et super
nobiles ascendunt : apud ceteros impares libertini liber-
tatis argumentum sunt.

Faenus agitare et in usuras extendere ignotum ; ideoque 26
magis servatur quam si vetitum esset. Agri pro numero
cultorum ab universis in vices occupantur, quos mox inter
se secundum dignationem partiuntur ; facilitatem par-
tiendi camporum spatia praestant. Arva per annos 5
mutant, et superest ager. Nec enim cum ubertate et
amplitudine soli labore contendunt, ut pomaria conserant
et prata separent et hortos rigent : sola terrae seges imperatur. Vnde annum quoque ipsum non in totidem
digerunt species : hiems et ver et aestas intellectum 10

ac vocabula habent, autumni perinde nomen ac bona
ignorantur.

27   Funerum nulla ambitio : id solum observatur, ut
corpora clarorum virorum certis lignis crementur.   Struem
rogi nec vestibus nec odoribus cumulant : sua cuique arma,
quorundam igni et equus adicitur.   Sepulcrum caespes
5 erigit : monumentorum arduum et operosum honorem ut
gravem defunctis aspernantur.   Lamenta ac lacrimas cito,
dolorem et tristitiam tarde ponunt.   Feminis lugere hones-
tum est, viris meminisse.

Haec in commune de omnium Germanorum origine ac
10 moribus accepimus : nunc singularum gentium instituta
ritusque, quatenus differant, quae nationes e Germania
in Gallias commigraverint, expediam.

28   Validiores olim Gallorum res fuisse summus auctorum
divus Iulius tradit ; eoque credibile est etiam Gallos in
Germaniam transgressos : quantulum enim amnis ob-
stabat quo minus, ut quaeque gens evaluerat, occuparet
5 permutaretque sedes promiscuas adhuc et nulla regnorum
potentia divisas ?   Igitur inter Hercyniam silvam Rhenumque et Moenum amnes Helvetii, ulteriora Boii, Gallica
utraque gens, tenuere.   Manet adhuc Boihaemi nomen
significatque loci veterem memoriam quamvis mutatis
10 cultoribus.   Sed utrum Aravisci in Pannoniam ab Osis,
Germanorum natione, an Osi ab Araviscis in Germaniam
commigraverint, cum eodem adhuc sermone institutis
moribus utantur, incertum est, quia pari olim inopia
ac libertate eadem utriusque ripae bona malaque erant.
15 Treveri et Nervii circa adfectationem Germanicae originis
ultro ambitiosi sunt, tamquam per hanc gloriam sanguinis
a similitudine et inertia Gallorum separentur.   Ipsam
Rheni ripam haud dubie Germanorum populi colunt,

Vangiones, Triboci, Nemetes. Ne Ubii quidem, quamquam Romana colonia esse meruerint ac libentius Agrip- 20
pinenses conditoris sui nomine vocentur, origine erube-
scnnt, transgressi olim et experimento fidei super ipsam
Rheni ripam conlocati, ut arcerent, non ut custodirentur.

Omnium harum gentium virtute praecipui Batavi non 29
multum ex ripa, sed insulam Rheni amnis colunt, Chattorum quondam populus et seditione domestica in eas
sedes transgressus, in quibus pars Romani imperii fierent.
Manet bonos et antiquae societatis insigne; nam nec 5
tributis contemnuntur nec publicanus atterit; exempti
oneribus et conlationibus et tantum in usum proeliorum
sepositi, velut tela atque arma, bellis reservantur. Est
in eodem obsequio et Mattiacorum gens; protulit enim
magnitudo populi Romani ultra Rhenum ultraque veteres 10
terminos imperii reverentiam. Ita sede finibusque in
sua ripa, mente animoque nobiscum agunt, cetera similes
Batavis, nisi quod ipso adhuc terrae suae solo et caelo
acrius animantur.

Non numeraverim inter Germaniae populos, quamquam 15
trans Rhenum Danuviumque consederint, eos qui decumates agros exercent. Levissimus quisque Gallorum et
inopia audax dubiae possessionis solum occupavere; mox
limite acto promotisque praesidiis sinus imperii et pars
provinciae habentur. 20

Ultra hos Chatti initium sedis ab Hercynio saltu inco- 30
hant, non ita effusis ac palustribus locis, ut ceterae civitates, in quas Germania patescit; durant siquidem
colles, paulatim rarescunt, et Chattos suos saltus Hercynius
prosequitur simul atque deponit. Duriora genti corpora, 5
stricti artus, minax vultus et maior animi vigor. Multum,
ut inter Germanos, rationis ac sollertiae: praeponere

electos, audire praepositos, nosse ordines, intellegere oc
casiones, differre impetus, disponere diem, vallare noctem,
10 fortunam inter dubia, virtutem inter certa numerare,
quodque rarissimum nec nisi ratione disciplinae concessum, plus reponere in duce quam in exercitu. Omne robur
in pedite, quem super arma ferramentis quoque et copiis
onerant : alios ad proelium ire videas, Chattos ad bellum.
15 Rari excursus et fortuita pugna. Equestrium sane
virium id proprium, cito parare victoriam, cito cedere :
velocitas iuxta formidinem, cunctatio propior constantiae
est.

31 Et aliis Germanorum populis usurpatum raro et privata
cuiusque audentia apud Chattos in consensum vertit, ut
primum adoleverint, crinem barbamque submittere, nec
nisi hoste caeso exuere votivum obligatumque virtuti
5 oris habitum. Super sanguinem et spolia revelant frontem, seque tum demum pretia nascendi rettulisse dignos-
que patria ac parentibus ferunt : ignavis et imbellibus
manet squalor. Fortissimus quisque ferreum insuper
anulum (ignominiosum id genti) velut vinculum gestat,
10 donec se caede hostis absolvat. Plurimis Chattorum hic
placet habitus, iamque canent insignes et hostibus simul
suisque monstrati. Omnium penes hos initia pugnarum ;
haec prima semper acies, visu nova ; nam ne in pace
quidem vultu mitiore mansuescunt. Nulli domus aut
15 ager aut aliqua cura : prout ad quemque venere, aluntur,
prodigi alieni, contemptores sui, donec exsanguis senectus
tam durae virtuti impares faciat.

32 Proximi Chattis certum iam alveo Rhenum, quique
terminus esse sufficiat, Usipi ac Tencteri colunt. Tencteri
super solitum bellorum decus equestris disciplinae arte
praecellunt ; nec maior apud Chattos peditum laus

quam Tencteris equitum. Sic instituere maiores ; posteri 5
imitantur. Hi lusus infantium, haec iuvenum aemulatio :
perseverant senes. Inter familiam et penates et iura
successionum equi traduntur : excipit filius, non ut cetera,
maximus natu, sed prout ferox bello et melior.

Iuxta Tencteros Bructeri olim occurrebant : nunc 33
Chamavos et Angrivarios inmigrasse narratur, pulsis
Bructeris ac penitus excisis vicinarum consensu nationum,
seu superbiae odio seu praedae dulcedine seu favore
quodam erga nos deorum ; nam ne spectaculo quidem 5
proelii invidere. Super sexaginta milia non armis telisque
Romanis, sed, quod magnificentius est, oblectationi oculisque ceciderunt. Maneat, quaeso, duretque gentibus,
si non amor nostri, at certe odium sui, quando urgentibus
imperii fatis nihil iam praestare fortuna maius potest 10
quam hostium discordiam.

Angrivarios et Chamavos a tergo Dulgubnii et Chasu- 34
arii cludunt, aliaeque gentes haud perinde memoratae, a
fronte Frisii excipiunt. Maioribus minoribusque Frisiis
vocabulum est ex modo virium. Utraeque nationes usque
ad Oceanum Rheno praetexuntur, ambiuntque inmensos 5
insuper lacus et Romanis classibus navigatos. Ipsum
quin etiam Occanum illa temptavimus : et superesse
adhuc Herculis columnas fama vulgavit, sive adiit
Hercules, seu quidquid ubique magnificum est, in clari-
tatem eius referre consensimus. Nec defuit audentia 10
Druso Germanico, sed obstitit Oceanus in se simul atque
in Herculem inquiri. Mox nemo temptavit, sanctiusque
ac reverentius visum de actis deorum credere quam scire.

Hactenus in occidentem Germaniam novimus ; in 35
septentrionem ingenti flexu redit. Ac primo statim Chaucorum gens, quamquam incipiat a Frisiis ac partem litoris

c

occupet, omnium quas exposui gentium lateribus obtendi-
5 tur, donec in Chattos usque sinuetur. Tam inmensum
terrarum spatium non tenent tantum Chauci, sed et im-
plent, populus inter Germanos nobilissimus, quique mag-
nitudinem suam malit iustitia tueri. Sine cupididate,
sine impotentia, quieti secretique nulla provocant bella,
10 nullis raptibus aut latrociniis populantur. Id praecipuum
virtutis ac virium argumentum est, quod, ut superiores
agant, non per iniurias adsequuntur; prompta tamen
omnibus arma ac, si res poscat, exercitus, plurimum virorum equorumque; et quiescentibus eadem fama.

36 In latere Chaucorum Chattorumque Cherusci nimiam
ac marcentem diu pacem inlacessiti nutrierunt : idque iu-
cundius quam tutius fuit, quia inter impotentes et validos
falso quiescas : ubi manu agitur, modestia ac probitas
5 nomina superioris sunt. Ita qui olim boni aequique
Cherusci, nunc inertes ac stulti vocantur : Chattis victori-
bus fortuna in sapientiam cessit. Tracti ruina Cherusco-
rum et Fosi, contermina gens. Adversarum rerum ex
aequo socii sunt, cum in secundis minores fuissent.

37 Eundem Germaniae sinum proximi Oceano Cimbri
tenent, parva nunc civitas, sed gloria ingens. Veterisque
famae lata vestigia manent, utraque ripa castra ac spatia,
quorum ambitu nunc quoque metiaris molem manusque
5 gentis et tam magni exitus fidem. Sescentesimum et
quadragesimum annum urbs nostra agebat, cum primum
Cimbrorum audita sunt arma, Caecilio Metello et
Papirio Carbone consulibus. Ex quo si ad alterum im-
peratoris Traiani consulatum computemus, ducenti
10 ferme et decem anni colliguntur : tam diu Germania vincitur. Medio tam longi aevi spatio multa in vicem damna.
Non Samnis, non Poeni, non Hispaniae Galliaeve, ne

Parthi quidem saepius admonuere: quippe regno Arsacis acrior est Germanorum libertas. Quid enim aliud nobis quam caedem Crassi, amisso et ipse Pacoro, infra 15 Ventidium deiectus Oriens obiecerit? At Germani Carbone et Cassio et Scauro Aurelio et Servilio Caepione Gnaeoque Mallio fusis vel captis quinque simul consularis exercitus populo Romano, Varum trisque cum eo legiones etiam Caesari abstulerunt; nec impune C. Marius in 20 Italia, divus Iulius in Gallia, Drusus ac Nero et Germanicus in suis eos sedibus perculerunt. Mox ingentes Gai Caesaris minae in ludibrium versae. Inde otium, donec occasione discordiae nostrae et civilium armorum expugnatis legionum hibernis etiam Gallias adfectavere; ac 25 rursus inde pulsi proximis temporibus triumphati magis quam victi sunt.

Nunc de Suebis dicendum est, quorum non una, ut 38 Chattorum Tencterorumve, gens; maiorem enim Germaniae partem obtinent, propriis adhuc nationibus nominibusque discreti, quamquam in commune Suebi vocentur. Insigne gentis obliquare crinem nodoque 5 substringere: sic Suebi a ceteris Germanis, sic Sueborum ingenui a servis separantur. In aliis gentibus seu cognatione aliqua Sueborum seu, quod saepe accidit, imitatione, rarum et intra iuventae spatium; apud Suebos usque ad canitiem horrentem capillum retro sequuntur. 10 Ac saepe in ipso vertice religatur; principes et ornatiorem habent. Ea cura formae, sed innoxia; neque enim ut ament amenturve, in altitudinem quandam et terrorem adituri bella compti, ut hostium oculis, armantur.

Vetustissimos se nobilissimosque Sueborum Semnones 39 memorant; fides antiquitatis religione firmatur. Stato tempore in silvam auguriis patrum et prisca formidine

sacram omnes eiusdem sanguinis populi legationibus
5 coëunt caesoque publice homine celebrant barbari ritus
horrenda primordia. Est et alia luco reverentia : nemo
nisi vinculo ligatus ingreditur, ut minor et potestatem
numinis prae se ferens. Si forte prolapsus est, attolli et
insurgere haud licitum : per humum evolvuntur. Eoque
10 omnis superstitio respicit, tamquam inde initia gentis,
ibi regnator omnium deus, cetera subiecta atque parentia.
Adicit auctoritatem fortuna Semnonum : centum pagi iis
habitantur magnoque corpore efficitur ut se Sueborum
caput credant.

40 Contra Langobardos paucitas nobilitat : plurimis ac
valentissimis nationibus cincti non per obsequium, sed
proeliis ac periclitando tuti sunt. Reudigni deinde et
Aviones et Anglii et Varini et Eudoses et Suardones et
5 Nuithones fluminibus aut silvis muniuntur. Nec quicquam
notabile in singulis, nisi quod in commune Nerthum, id est
Terram matrem, colunt eamque intervenire rebus hominum,
invehi populis arbitrantur. Est in insula Oceani castum
nemus, dicatumque in eo vehiculum, veste contectum ;
10 attingere uni sacerdoti concessum. Is adesse penetrali
deam intellegit vectamque bubus feminis multa cum vene-
ratione prosequitur. Laeti tunc dies, festa loca, quaecumque adventu hospitioque dignatur. Non bella ineunt,
non arma sumunt ; clausum omne ferrum ; pax et quies
15 tunc tantum nota, tunc tantum amata, donec idem sacerdos satiatam conversatione mortalium deam templo
reddat. Mox vehiculum et vestes et, si credere velis,
numen ipsum secreto lacu abluitur. Servi ministrant,
quos statim idem lacus haurit. Arcanus hinc terror
20 sanctaque ignorantia, quid sit illud, quod tantum perituri
vident.

Et haec quidem pars Sueborum in secretiora Germaniac **41**
porrigitur. Propior, ut, quo modo paulo ante Rhenum,
sic nunc Danuvium sequar, Hermundurorum civitas, fida
Romanis; eoque solis Germanorum non in ripa commer-
cium, sed penitus atque in splendidissima Raetiae pro- 5
vinciae colonia. Passim et sine custode transeunt; et
cum ceteris gentibus arma modo castraque nostra ostendamus, his domos villasque patefecimus non concupiscenti-
bus. In Hermunduris Albis oritur, flumen inclutum
et notum olim; nunc tantum auditur.   10

Iuxta Hermunduros Naristi ac deinde Marcomani et **42**
Quadi agunt. Praecipua Marcomanorum gloria viresque,
atque ipsa etiam sedes pulsis olim Boiis virtute parta.
Nec Naristi Quadive degenerant. Eaque Germaniae
velut frons est, quatenus Danuvio peragitur. Marco- 5
manis Quadisque usque ad nostram memoriam reges
mausere ex gente ipsorum, nobile Marobodui et Tudri
genus: iam et externos patiuntur, sed vis et potentia
regibus ex auctoritate Romana. Raro armis nostris,
saepius pecunia iuvantur, nec minus valent.   10

Retro Marsigni, Cotini, Osi, Buri terga Marcomanorum **43**
Quadorumque claudunt. E quibus Marsigni et Buri
sermone cultuque Suebos referunt: Cotinos Gallica,
Osos Pannonica lingua coarguit non esse Germanos, et
quod tributa patiuntur. Partem tributorum Sarmatae, 5
partem Quadi ut alienigenis imponunt: Cotini, quo magis
pudeat, et ferrum effodiunt. Omnesque hi populi pauca
campestrium, ceterum saltus et vertices montium iugumque
insederunt. Dirimit enim scinditque Suebiam continuum
montium iugum, ultra quod plurimae gentes agunt, ex 10
quibus latissime patet Lygiorum nomen in plures civitates
diffusum. Valentissimas nominasse sufficiet, Harios,

Helveconas, Manimos, Helisios, Nahanarvalos. Apud
Nahanarvalos antiquae religionis lucus ostenditur. Prae-
15 sidet sacerdos muliebri ornatu, sed deos interpretatione
Romana Castorem Pollucemque memorant. Ea vis
numini, nomen Alcis. Nulla simulacra, nullum peregrinae superstitionis vestigium; ut fratres tamen, ut
iuvenes venerantur. Ceterum Harii super vires, quibus
20 enumeratos paulo ante populos antecedunt, truces in-
sitae feritati arte ac tempore lenocinantur: nigra scuta,
tincta corpora; atras ad proelia noctes legunt ipsaque
formidine atque umbra feralis exercitus terrorem in-
ferunt, nullo hostium sustinente novum ac velut infer-
25 num adspectum; nam primi in omnibus proeliis oculi
vincuntur.

Trans Lygios Gotones regnantur, paulo iam adductius
quam ceterae Germanorum gentes, nondum tamen supra
libertatem. Protinus deinde ab Oceano Rugii et Lemovii;
30 omniumque harum gentium insigne rotunda scuta, breves
gladii et erga reges obsequium.

44 Suionum hinc civitates ipso in Oceano praeter viros
armaque classibus valent. Forma navium eo differt,
quod utrimque prora paratam semper adpulsui frontem
agit. Nec velis ministrantur nec remos in ordinem lateri-
5 bus adiungunt: solutum, ut in quibusdam fluminum,
et mutabile, ut res poscit, hinc vel illinc remigium. Est
apud illos et opibus honos, eoque unus imperitat, nullis
iam exceptionibus, non precario iure parendi. Nec arma,
ut apud ceteros Germanos, in promiscuo, sed clausa sub
10 custode, et quidem servo, quia subitos hostium incursus
prohibet Oceanus, otiosae porro armatorum manus facile
lasciviunt. Enimvero neque nobilem neque ingenuum,
ne libertinum quidem armis praeponere regia utilitas est.

Trans Suionas aliud mare, pigrum ac prope inmotum, 45
quo cingi cludique terrarum orbem hinc fides, quod extre-
mus cadentis iam solis fulgor in ortus edurat adeo clarus,
ut sidera hebetet; sonum insuper emergentis audiri
formasque equorum et radios capitis adspici persuasio 5
adicit. Illuc usque (et fama vera) tantum natura. Ergo
iam dextro Suebici maris litore Aestiorum gentes adluuntur,
quibus ritus habitusque Sueborum, lingua Britannicae
propior. Matrem deum venerantur. Insigne superstitionis formas aprorum gestant: id pro armis omniumque 10
tutela securum deae cultorem etiam inter hostis praestat.
Rarus ferri, frequens fustium usus. Frumenta ceterosque
fructus patientius quam pro solita Germanorum inertia
laborant. Sed et mare scrutantur, ac soli omnium
sucinum, quod ipsi glesum vocant, inter vada atque in 15
ipso litore legunt. Nec quae natura, quaeve ratio gignat,
ut barbaris, quaesitum compertumve; diu quin etiam
inter cetera eiectamenta maris iacebat, donec luxuria
nostra dedit nomen. Ipsis in nullo usu; rude legitur,
informe profertur, pretiumque mirantes accipiunt. Sucum 20
tamen arborum esse intellegas, quia terrena quaedam
atque etiam volucria animalia plerumque interlucent,
quae implicata umore mox durescente materia cluduntur.
Fecundiora igitur nemora lucosque sicut Orientis secretis,
ubi tura balsamaque sudantur, ita Occidentis insulis 25
terrisque inesse crediderim, quae vicini solis radiis expressa
atque liquentia in proximum mare labuntur ac vi tem-
pestatum in adversa litora exundant. Si naturam sucini
admoto igni temptes, in modum taedae accenditur alitque
flammam pinguem et olentem ; mox ut in picem resinamve 30
lentescit.
  Suionibus Sitonum gentes continuantur. Cetera similes

uno differunt, quod femina dominatur; in tantum non
modo a libertate sed etiam a servitute degenerant.

46 Hic Suebiae finis. Peucinorum Venedorumque et
Fennorum nationes Germanis an Sarmatis adscribam
dubito, quamquam Peucini, quos quidam Bastarnas
vocant, sermone, cultu, sede ac domiciliis ut Germani
5 agunt. Sordes omnium ac torpor procerum; conubiis
mixtis nonnihil in Sarmatarum habitum foedantur.
Venedi multum ex moribus traxerunt; nam quidquid inter
Peucinos Fennosque silvarum ac montium erigitur latrociniis pererrant. Hi tamen inter Germanos potius re-
10 feruntur, quia et domos figunt et scuta gestant et pedum
usu ac pernicitate gaudent: quae omnia diversa Sarmatis
sunt in plaustro equoque viventibus. Fennis mira feritas,
foeda paupertas: non arma, non equi, non penates;
victui herba, vestitui pelles, cubile humus: solae in
15 sagittis spes, quas inopia ferri ossibus asperant. Idemque
venatus viros pariter ac feminas alit; passim enim comitantur partemque praedae petunt. Nec· aliud infantibus
ferarum imbriumque suffugium quam ut in aliquo ramorum
nexu contegantur: huc redeunt iuvenes, hoc senum re-
20 ceptaculum. Sed beatius arbitrantur quam ingemere
agris, inlaborare domibus, suas alienasque fortunas spe
metuque versare: securi adversus homines, securi adversus deos rem difficillimam adsecuti sunt, ut illis ne voto
quidem opus esset. Cetera iam fabulosa: Hellusios et
25 Oxionas ora hominum voltusque, corpora atque artus
ferarum gerere: quod ego ut incompertum in medio
relinquam.

NOTES

Chapter 1.

The boundaries of Germany; the courses of the Rhine and the Danube.

1. Germania omnis: *Germany as a whole;* Tacitus echoes the opening words of Caesar's *Bellum Gallicum.* Germany proper is here considered as a geographical unit apart from the Roman provinces of Upper and Lower Germany, which were situated on the left bank of the Rhine. — **Raetisque et Pannoniis**: these nouns, connected by *et,* stand in close relation as the second member of the coördinate series. The Raeti inhabited Eastern Switzerland, the Tyrol, and Southern Bavaria.

The western boundary of Pannonia lay somewhat to the west of Vienna; on the north and the east the province was bordered by the Danube. Between Raetia and Pannonia lay Noricum, which Tacitus here leaves unmentioned.

2. Sarmātis: peoples containing Slavic elements and also possessing racial affinity with the Medes and Persians; their domain in general comprised the steppes of Russia north of the Black Sea and the Caucasus Mountains. One tribe, the Iazyges, occupied at this time that part of Hungary that lies between the Danube and the Theiss. — **Dacisque**: a Thracian stock which, a decade before the *Germania* was written, had inflicted severe defeats on the armies of Domitian; Transylvania and adjacent regions were included in Dacian territory. — **mutuo metu aut montibus**: a striking example of the combination of concrete and abstract ideas; cf. the note on *Agricola* 25. 8. This usage is favored especially by Tacitus and the poets of the Empire; one of the earliest instances in Latin is Plautus, *Rudens* 436 · *nostro illum puteum periclo et ferramentis fodimus* (' I dug that well with peril to myself and with iron tools '). The mountains referred to are the Carpathians.

3. Oceanus: the North Sea and the Baltic. — **sinus**: used here, as in *Agricola* 23. 6 and *Germania* 37. 1, in the sense of a ' projection of the land.'

4. insularum: including the Scandinavian Peninsula, regarded for centuries after Tacitus as an island. — **nuper**: this word may be extended in meaning to include an event not too remote in the past; cf. the indefiniteness of our expression " in modern times " and the extensibility of such Latin words as *antiquitus, vetus*, et. cet. See note on *Agricola* 1. 2. The furthest advance of Roman forces in these regions was achieved in 5 A.D., when an expedition under the command of Tiberius penetrated as far as the Cattegat. Roman fleets also operated along the German coast of the North Sea in 12 B.C. under Drusus and in 15 and 16 A.D. under Germanicus. — **cognitis . . . gentibus**: a loose ablative absolute construction, added to justify the assertion made with reference to the vast extent of the peninsulas and islands.

5. aperuit: cf. the similar metaphor in *Agricola* 22. 1: *tertius annus . . . novas gentis aperuit.*

6. vertice ortus: the Rhine proper is actually formed by the confluence of two tributaries, the ' Hinter ' Rhine and the ' Vorder ' Rhine, which rise in different parts of the Swiss canton Grisons. The source of the Vorder Rhine is near St. Gotthard, ancient Adula, the *vertex* here referred to.

7. versus: a participle, reflexive in force.

8. molli et clementer edito: cf. our English expression " a gentle slope "; there is a contrast with *inaccesso ac praecipiti*.

9. Abnŏbae: the name applied in ancient times to the Black Forest. The source of the Danube is on the eastern slope. — **pluris**: here equivalent to *compluris*.

10. donec . . . erumpat: as is not infrequent in late Latin, *donec* introduces a subjunctive in a statement of fact where classical usage would demand an indicative. — **septimum os**: almost without exception, Greek writers, from the time of Herodotus on, assigned five mouths to the Danube. Among the Romans, traditional computation after the Augustan age declared for seven, which the fame of the Nile Delta rendered a favored number for rivers' mouths. Thus Vergil, *Aeneid* 9. 30, ascribes seven outlets to the Ganges. As a matter of fact the Danube, before entering the Black Sea, divides into three branches, the Kilia, the Sulina, and the St. George's; the Kilia discharges through seven channels and the St. George's through two.

11. paludibus: the whole delta is marshland and covers an area of 1000 sq. m.

Chapter 2.

The origin of the German race; its reputed progenitors; extension of the name.

1. ipsos: as in *Agricola* 13. 1, the pronoun marks a transition from physical geography to peoples.

2. hospitiis: *as a result of relations of hospitality* (established with non-German peoples). — **terra**: zeugma with *advehebantur* is involved; supply *adveniebant*.

3. olim: *in primitive times.* — **classibus advehebantur**: Tacitus's rejection of the possibility of folk migration by land is, of course, out of keeping with the facts of history. He had especially in mind the mythological traditions as to the wanderings of the peoples of the Mediterranean Basin, *e.g.* Greeks, Trojans, and Phoenicians.

4. ultra: used attributively, as in *Agricola* 30. 16: *nulla iam ultra gens.* Translate: *beyond the limits of the known world.* — **adversus**: *lying over against us.* The word does not necessitate the assumption of an allusion to the spherical shape of the earth, a view which Tacitus did not accept, as is clear from *Agricola* 12. The Ocean is in imagination transferred to a separate quarter of the earth fronting the known world; it is a hyperbole common among Roman writers to refer to a remote clime as ' another world '; Pliny, *Natural History* 4. (27). 96: *clarissima est Scadinavia incompertae magnitudinis quae* (i.e. *Hillevionum gens) alterum orbem terrarum eam appellat* (' most famous (of these islands) is Scadinavia, (a land) of unknown vastness, . . . the race of the Hilleviones calls it another world '); sometimes, as in this passage, the boldness of the conception is tempered by the insertion of a limiting word or clause; thus Velleius Paterculus, a historian of the time of Tiberius, writes in 2. 46. 1: *cum in Britanniam traiecisset exercitum, alterum paene . . . quaerens orbem* (' when . . . he had transported his army to Britain, in quest of what is well nigh another world ').

7. informem: lit. *shapeless*, hence here applied to the savage aspect of an uncultivated land. The Romans had little taste for the picturesque and the wild in natural scenery.

8. tristem cultu adspectuque: *gloomy to dwell in and to view.* — **nisi si patria sit:** an oft-repeated sentiment; cf. Cicero, *De Amicitia* 68: *consuetudo valet, cum locis ipsis delectemur, montuosis etiam et silvestribus, in quibus diutius commorati sumus* ('familiarity has its effect, in that we find delight in the very country, mountainous and wooded even though it be, in which we have sojourned a longer time than usual'); James Montgomery's lines:

> " Man through all ages of revolving time,
> Unchanging man in every varying clime,
> Deems his own land of every land the pride,
> Beloved of Heaven o'er all the world beside."

9. carminibus antiquis: sagas, or lays dealing with the genealogies and deeds of heroes, such as preceded prose history writing among the Greeks and probably among the Romans. — **quod unum . . . annalium genus:** in the case of the Britons, Tacitus was unable to cite explicitly even poetic tradition as to their origin; cf. *Agricola* 11. 2.

10. Tuistonem: *i.e.* ' the twofold one '; compare Ger. *zwei*, *zwischen*; Eng. *two*. He may have been conceived of as bisexual; an interesting, though not a complete, analogy is Cecrops, mythical founder of the royal line of Athens, who, as did Tuisto, sprang from the earth and was portrayed as *biformis*, half man and half serpent.

11. Mannum: *i.e.* ' the thinking creature,' derived from the root which appears in Gk. μιμνήσκω, Lat. *memini*, Ger. *Mensch*, Eng. *man*. Mannus was thus the first human being endowed with the power of thought. There is reason to believe that we have here the Germanic offshoot of the Indo-European myth of the creation of man.

12. tris filios: three sons are characteristic of the third generation in mythical genealogies; thus, Uranus, Cronus, and Zeus, Poseidon, Pluto; Deucalion (the Greek Noah), Hellen, and Dorus, Xuthus, Aeolus. We may recall in this connection Shem, Ham, and Japheth, the " three sons of Noah and of them was the whole earth overspread." It is possible that Mannus was the Germanic Noah. — e quorum nominibus : the names of these eponymous ancestors have been reconstructed as Ingvas or Ing, Erminas or Irmin, and Istvas. Note the alliteration characteristic of such groups of gods or heroes in Germanic myth. Around each of the three centered a cult group consisting of peoples supposedly united by ties of relationship in their common descent from the heroic forefather. In the process of religious development the worship of some one of the chief gods of the German pantheon became dominant among the tribes composing each of the three groups, although not necessarily restricted to the group or adopted by all the tribes in it. Thus the cults of Freyr and Tiu flourished especially among the Ingaevones and the Herminones respectively ; the worship of Wodan had its center in the regions occupied by the Istaevones. In each case the original eponymous hero tended to merge with the personality of the greater divinity and the name of the progenitor to become an epithet of the god.

This classification into three races does not pretend to be complete and is not utilized by Tacitus in his detailed discussion of German ethnology, chap. 28 and following. Hence it should not be assumed that he meant to imply that these three groups included all the peoples of Germany. He is concerned here chiefly with the mythical genealogy of the Germans and so singles out for mention these three divisions as being those which, according to the tradition of the Germans themselves, preserved in their names proof of origin from the sons of Mannus, the common ancestor. Therefore he deemed it necessary to locate them only roughly. As a matter of fact, this classification applies only to the peoples west of the Oder. Pliny, *Natural History* 4. (28). 99, gives a more comprehensive, though not exhaustive, division of the races of Germany, in which he adds to the three groups here mentioned the Vandili of Northeastern Germany and the Peucini along the eastern border.

13. Ingaevŏnes : Pliny's transcription, *Ingvaeones*, is closer to the original German than the spelling of Tacitus, which has been modified to suit Roman vocal organs. Modern scholars differ as to the transliteration of all three names.

This group included especially the inhabitants of the Danish Peninsula, *e.g.* the Cimbri and the Teutons; the Anglo-Saxons are assigned by some scholars to the Ingaevones, by others to the Herminones. **Herminŏnes**: comprising peoples which dwelt on the east and the west of the Upper Elbe, as the Langobardi, the Semnones, the Chatti, the Cherusci, and the Hermunduri. The Hessians and the Thuringians of later times sprang from this group.

14. Istaevŏnes: transliterated more accurately by Pliny, Istvaeones. They numbered among them the tribes which occupied the territory along the Lower Rhine, such as the Sugambri, Batavi, Chamavi, Ubii, Usipi, and were the forefathers of the Franks of West Germany and Holland.

The specimens of pottery and the numerous articles of bronze and iron work which have been unearthed in the sepulchral mounds found in the regions once occupied by the Istaevones and the Herminones, indicate that the latter peoples reached a higher degree of civilization than the former. The Istaevones seem deliberately to have resisted the more advanced culture of their Celtic neighbors. — **quidam**: Roman scholars and writers, whose views are continued in chap. 3. — **ut in licentia vetustatis**: *as is to be expected in connection with the freedom of opinion attaching itself to matters of the remote past.*

15. pluris deo ortos: a much discussed passage, best explained as follows: *more (than three) descendants of the god* (i.e. *Tuisto*). — **gentis appellationes**: *race names.* The four names following are cited as examples only and are not intended as a complete list. We may be certain that the names of the eponymous ancestors not mentioned here were invented by Roman authorities or German informants, to account for existing tribal names. This was the usual ætiological practice of the ancients; cf. Hellenes, from a mythical Hellen, Ionians from Ion. — **Marsos**: a branch of the Sugambri; they suffered severely in the campaigns waged by Germanicus in 14 A.D. against the peoples dwelling near the Lippe and the Ruhr, and subsequently dispersed into the interior.

16. Gambrivios: they also lived in Western Germany, in the vicinity of the Cherusci and the Chatti. Kinship with the Sugambri is indicated by the presence of the root *gambr-* in both names. — **Suebos**: the application of this name was subject to variation on the part of Roman writers. As used here by Tacitus, it embraces the Semnones, Chatti, and other tribes of Southern and Western Germany, living on and about the Elbe. In chap. 38 we shall see that the peoples included under the name were much more widely extended. — **Vandilios**: originally applied, as in Pliny, *Natural History* 4. (28). 99 and in this passage, to an ethnic division comprising many peoples of Eastern Germany, the name, in its later form *Vandali*, was restricted to the tribe famous in the period of the Germanic migrations into the Empire. — **eaque vera . . . nomina**: supply *esse;* the indirect discourse continues to the end of the chapter.

17. ceterum: *whereas (they assert).* The conjunction introduces a contrast between *vera et antiqua nomina* and *vocabulum recens* et cet.

18. primi Rhenum transgressi Gallos expulerint: in close agreement with Caesar, *Bellum Gallicum* 2. 4. 1, who asserts that most of the Belgae were descended from Germanic invaders who, tempted by the fertility of the soil, had crossed the Rhine and ejected the Celtic inhabitants. *Antiquitus* is the word used by Caesar to define the date of this migration; it was at least prior to the incursion of the Cimbri and the Teutons. The Remi furnished Caesar with the data for this part of his narrative; however, there seems to be no ground for distrusting the accuracy of the account, although elsewhere in the *Gallic War* the reliability of information derived from native sources is open to question.

19. ac nunc Tungri, tunc Germani: according to Caesar, *Bellum Gallicum* 2. 4. 10, a confederation of four tribes of Belgic Gaul, the Condrusi, Eburones, Caerosi, and Caemani, bore collectively the name *Germani*. A view which has gained wide acceptance is that this was the term applied by the Celts to the Teutonic intruders. Its etymology is uncertain. The accuracy of the statement of Tacitus, that peoples once called Germani were in his time known as Tungri, is substantiated by the fact that, in the first century of the Empire, Tungri occupied the territory adjacent to 'Aduatuca, once the chief city of Caesar's Eburones (Germani), and later called Aduatuca Tongrorum, surviving in modern Tongres near Liège. Tungri served in Agricola's army in Britain; cf. *Agricola* 36. 5.

20. nationis nomen . . . evaluisse: in history instances are plentiful in which the name of a tribe (the sense of *natio* here) has been extended over a whole race or people; cf. the extension of the name *Hellenes*, originally a Thessalian tribe. The French word *Allemand* is derived from the name of a single race, the *Alamanni*.

21. omnes: the main body of the Germans who still remained in their own domain on the right bank of the Rhine. — **a victore ob metum:** the original Teutonic invaders, in order to overawe the conquered Celts, applied the name bestowed on themselves to their compatriots across the Rhine. They would thus inspire the belief among the Gauls that others of the same race as themselves, hence just as formidable foemen, stood ready to cross and assist them to hold what they had gained. This interpretation of a difficult passage understands *ob metum* in an active sense, as equivalent to *ob metum iniciendum*. — **a se ipsis:** subsequently the name received universal sanction among the Germans. Recall that it is the view of Roman critics (*quidam*) that Tacitus is still expounding. In point of fact, it is scarcely credible that at this period the Germans had adopted for themselves any collective racial designation, comparable to the later *Deutsch*, which became established in the eleventh century A.D. It was only among the Romans and the Gauls that the generic name *Germani* had currency.   .

Chapter 3.

Hercules and Ulysses among the Germans; German war-songs.

1. et: the Germans had various native heroes. Hercules *also*, a hero of foreign origin, sojourned among them. — **Herculem:** in this passage Tacitus has blended two separate ideas: (1) a myth as to the presence in Germany, on some one of his peregrinations, of the Hercules of Greek and Roman mythology. Similarly, we are informed below of a tradition according to which the Greek Ulysses penetrated to Germany. (2) Beginning with *primumque*, Hercules is merged in the German god Donar or Thor, after the fashion, usual with Greek and Roman writers, of identifying, on the basis of resemblances in attribute or function, foreign divinities with gods of their own pantheon.   Thus Caesar found Mercury, Apollo, and Mars in Gaul, *Bellum Gallicum* 6. 17.

Hercules and Thor both fought with monsters, both were benefactors of mankind ; Thor's weapon, the hammer, suggested the club of Hercules. — memorant : alluding to Greek or Roman literary sources. — primum : *the original hero of them all.*

2. canunt : the subject has changed abruptly.

3. haec quoque carmina : mention of the battle-hymn celebrating the deeds of Donar suggested a digression dealing with a chant of a different type, but also sung as a prelude to the conflict.   *Haec = talia.* — relatu : *by the rendition.* — barditum : a Latinized German word, the etymology of which is uncertain. It has been connected with *bardhi*, ' shield,' and *bard, bart*, ' beard,' *bartrede* being an imitation of the hoarse utterance of Donar, the god of the thunder.

5. ipso cantu : *by the mere sound*, irrespective of the content of the song.

6. sonuit acies : cf. the description of the attack of Civilis and the Batavi on the Romans, *Historiae* 4. 18 : *ut virorum cantu, feminarum ululatu, sonuit acies* (' while the line resounded with the chanting of the men and the whoops of the women '). — nec tam vocis ille quam virtutis concentus : seek to render the rhetorical features of the diction by some such translation as : *a harmony not so much of voices as of valiant hearts.*

7. fractum murmur : *a pulsating roar.*   The reverberation from the shields would give the sound a muffled and tremulous quality.

9. ceterum : taking up the thread of the narrative proper after the digression.   Translate : *to resume.* — quidam : Greek and Roman antiquarians and writers ; ancient savants were given to extending the wanderings of Ulysses to any land where his presence would most plausibly account for the name of a city or for the existence of some local monument.   Here both motives were present.

10. fabuloso : *faméd in story*, as Horace, *Odes* 1. 22. 7 : *fabulosus .   . Hydaspes,* — or *fraught with legends.* — hunc Oceanum :

D

the North Sea ; Tacitus projects in thought the reader and himself
to the region which he is describing.

11. Asciburgium: a military post on the left bank of the
Lower Rhine. The name perhaps survives in the modern
Asberg, situated north of Cologne, near Düsseldorf.

12. hodieque: = *hodie quoque, even to this day.*

13. nominatum: Tacitus does not present the etymological
details on which the theory rested. These were doubtless fanci-
ful enough, since the demands of ancient philologists in such
respects were easily satisfied. Perhaps they saw in the name a
reminiscence of the famous bag (ἀσκός) in which Aeolus impris-
oned the unfavorable winds, *Odyssey* 10. 19–29. — **Ulixi**: best
explained as a dative of agent; an altar dedicated to Ulysses
would constitute no definitive proof of his stay.

15. Graecis litteris inscriptos: according to Caesar, *Bellum
Gallicum* 1. 29 and 6. 14, the Helvetians and the Druids were
acquainted with the Greek alphabet. The inscriptions here
referred to were probably written in an alphabet which archaeological discoveries made in the Tyrol have shown was in use
among the Raetians, and was closely akin to the Etruscan
alphabet.

18. ex ingenio suo: *according to his especial bent.*

Chapter 4.

The purity of the German stock ; the resultant uniformity of
physical type and characteristics.

2. nullis aliis aliarum nationum: i.e. *nullis conubiis aliis
aliarum nationum.* Tacitus emphasizes as strongly as possible
the freedom with which exogamy would have been practiced, if
it had been indulged in at all. Translate: *by no intermarriages,
promiscuously contracted with various races.* — **infectos**: *con-
taminated*: some editors attach to the word the milder connotation, *modified.*

4. tamquam . . . numero: *so far as can be judged in the case
of so great a population.*

5. truces et caerulei oculi: the Gauls assured Caesar's soldiers
that the mien and the glances of the Germans struck terror to
the hearts of their antagonists, *Bellum Gallicum* 1. 39. 1 ; *caeruleus*

is the standing word of description applied in Latin to the color of the eyes of the Germans; cf. Horace, *Epodes* 16. 7 and Juvenal, *Satires* 13. 164.

6. rutilae comae: the same characteristic is attributed to the Caledonians, *Agricola* 11. 4. — **magna corpora**: cf. *Agricola* 11. 4; Caesar, *Bellum Gallicum* 1. 39. 1 : *ingenti magnitudine corporum Germanos.* The large frames of the Gauls and the Germans were always a source of wonder to the shorter, more stocky Romans. — **tantum ad impetum valida**: in *Annales* 2. 14 Germanicus is represented as encouraging his soldiers before a battle with the assurance: *iam corpus (Germanorum) ut visu torvum et ad brevem impetum validum, sic nulla vulnerum patientia* et seq. (' moreover, the (German) physique, while grim to behold and powerful in a brief onset, has no capability in enduring wounds ').

7. non eadem: *not on a par* with their aggressiveness.

8. aestumque tolerare: in *Historiae* 2. 93 we are told that the heat of the Roman summer, and a reckless recourse to the waters of the Tiber, played havoc with the health of the German and Gallic troops of Vitellius. — **frigora atque inediam**: the force of *tolerare* is continued with these words; note the chiastic arrangement with reference to the preceding pair. The asyndeton conceals an adversative conjunction, as in *Agricola* 12. 18: *tarde mitescunt, cito proveniunt.*

9. caelo solove: causal ablatives. These words dexterously mark the transition to the description of the country and the products with which the next chapter begins.

Chapter 5.

The country and its products; the precious metals and the valuation attached to them.

1. aliquanto: *to some extent.*

2. silvis: according to Caesar, *Bellum Gallicum* 6. 25, the Hercynian Forest was nine days' journey in width and so long that a march of sixty days would not bring a traveler to its furthest borders. Other forests were the Teutoburgiensis, Bacensis, and Caesia. — **paludibus**: the typical description of the German terrain always contains reference to the marshes; e.g. *Historiae* 4. 73: *eadem semper causa Germanis transcendendi*

in Galliam   *ut relictis paludibus et solitudinibus suis fecundis-*
simum hoc solum   *possiderent* (' an always invariable reason
moved the Germans to cross into Gaul . . . (the desire) to leave
behind their native swamps and wildernesses and occupy this
highly fertile soil '). — **umidior qua Gallias**: not primarily a
direct allusion to a heavier rainfall, but to the swampy nature of
the country in West Germany and Holland, the scenes of most
of the Roman campaigns in Germany in the first century A.D.
Cf. Tacitus, *Annales* 1. 61, *umido paludum;* 1. 68, *egressos
per umida et impedita;* 2. 23, *umidis Germaniae terris.*

3. ventosior: contrasted with *umidior*, since the prevalence of
winds would make for a drier country. — **adspicit:** cf. *Agricola*
24. 3–4: *eamque partem Britanniae quae Hiberniam adspicit.* —
satis: ablative.

4. frugiferarum arborum inpatiens: written from the point
of view of one familiar with the opposite conditions existing in
Italy.   Total absence of fruit trees is not implied but only of their
cultivation; hence there is no inconsistency involved in the
mention of *agrestia poma* in chap. 23. 3.

5. improcera: supply *sunt pecora.* — **armentis:** *horned cattle.*
— **suus honor:** *their generic attractions,* referring especially to
size and appearance.

6. gloria frontis: flowery diction — *proud adornment of the
brow.*   They were not hornless, but lacked the branching horns
seen on Italian cattle to this day. — **numero:** instead of in fine
breeds. — **solae et gratissimae opes:** *solae* is a somewhat ex-
aggerated statement; *gratissimae* is more exact.   In certain
Old Germanic languages the same word signified ' cattle ' and
' wealth '; similarly, in Latin, *pecunia* is connected etymologically with *pecus.*   In the Homeric poems values are sometimes
expressed in terms of cattle, *e.g. Iliad* 2. 449 and 6. 236 ἑκατόμβοιος,
Odyssey 1. 431 ἐεικοσάβοιος.

7. propitii: the sentiment that " money is the root of all
evil " is as hackneyed in ancient literature as in modern ; *e.g.*
Vergil, *Aeneid* 3. 56: *Quid non mortalia pectora cogis, auri sacra
fames!* Propertius, 3. 13. 49–50:

> *auro pulsa fides, auro venalia iura,*
> *aurum lex sequitur, mox sine lege pudor*

(' gold has banished honor, gold purchases Justice's decrees, law follows in the train of gold, and anon the sense of shame, once law is gone ').

9. nullam Germaniae venam: over fifteen years later, when Tacitus was writing the *Annals*, he had learned of the presence of small deposits of silver near modern Wiesbaden ; cf. *Annales* 11. 20: *in agro Mattiaco recluserat (Curtius Rufus) specus quaerendis venis argenti* et seq. (' in the territory of the Mattiaci Curtius Rufus had opened up mines in a quest for veins of silver ').

10. haud perinde: *not especially;* literally there is an elliptical comparison, *ac aliae nationes* or the like, as in *Agricola* 10. 21.

11. est videre: like the Greek ἔστιν ὁρᾶν.

12. principibus: here used in a broad sense, *i.e. headmen,* including chieftains and kings.

13. quae humo finguntur: unlike the *argentea vasa*, the earthenware was of domestic origin. We have learned from the excavation of prehistoric tombs that the Germans had a pottery technique reaching back to very primitive times. — **quamquam**: *and yet;* the clause limits the preceding sentence. — **proximi**: *i.e.* to the Roman frontier. The numismatic finds amply confirm the assertion of Tacitus that, in his time, only the Germans who lived close to the boundaries had coins, and that these were exclusively of Republican mintage.

15. formas: *types.* — **adgnoscunt**: *they know well.*

17. probant: *they welcome.*

18. serratos bigatosque: supply *nummos;* the coins here referred to are two types of the silver denarius, which were not issued after the middle of the first century B.C. The former had milled edges, the latter was stamped with the picture of a *biga* or two-horsed chariot. Besides the natural partiality of peoples in any age for currency of a long-established value (compare the standing of the English sovereign and the French Napoleon nowadays), another reason for the Germans' preference lay in the fact that in the time of the Empire, notably after Nero, the denarius was debased with a bronze alloy.

19. adfectione animi: *penchant.*

20. facilior usui: *more serviceable;* the right " change," as we say, could be made more easily with a large number of coins of small denominations. — **promiscua**: *common wares.*

Chapter 6.

Weapons; military tactics and formations; the code of honor.

1. ne ferrum quidem: mention of the precious metals is logically succeeded by reference to iron among the Germans, and this forms an easy transition to the following description of arms and warfare. — **superest**: *is present in abundance.* Remains found in mounds in the region of the Elbe would indicate that, at least among the peoples of this locality, iron was present in large quantities.

2. rari gladiis: *rari* is not to be taken with strict literalness; the use of the sword was merely relatively less frequent than that of the *framea* (see below). In chap. 18 the sword is mentioned as a usual article of the marriage dower; the use of short swords was a racial characteristic of the East Germans; cf. chap. 43. Thus swords were scarcely a rarity in primitive Germany, taken by and large. They may, however, have been seen but seldom in the hands of the tribes of West Germany and it was with these that the Romans came in closest contact. — **lanceis**: these had stout shafts, broad iron heads, and were used only for thrusting.

3. frameas: the *framea*, styled by Tacitus except in this treatise simply *hasta*, was the characteristic national weapon of the Germans. In comparison with the *pilum* of the Romans the shaft seemed excessively long and the iron head short. In Christian literature *framea* means ' sword '; thus in the Latin Bible it is the regular equivalent for ῥομφαία. Cf. the analogous development in meaning of ἔγχος, in Homer ' spear,' in the tragedians ' sword.'

5. vel comminus vel eminus: notwithstanding the words of Tacitus here, there was a limit to the effectiveness of the *framea* at close quarters; cf. *Annales* 2. 21: (*Germani*) . . . *genere pugnae et armorum superabantur, cum ingens multitudo artis locis praelongas hastas non protenderet, non colligeret* (' the Germans were put at a disadvantage by the nature of the combat and the style of weapons employed, since, fighting in an immense crowd in a confined space, they could not thrust forward their very long lances and could not recover them ').

6. scuto: the German shields were made of wicker or of thin boards, sometimes reënforced with hide. Among the East Germans they were round in shape, elsewhere they were rectangular or hexagonal.

7. missilia: not only light javelins, but also stones and slung-shots. — **in inmensum**: *to an enormous distance.*

8. nudi aut sagulo leves: *nudus*, as well as the Greek γυμνός, is frequently used in the modified sense seen in our expression, " stripped for action." The German infantry removed all encumbering outer garments or else the light mantle that they wore left their movements unimpeded. — **cultus iactatio**: *ostentatiousness in equipment.*

9. coloribus: in Plutarch, *Marius* 25, we read of the white shields of the Cimbri; the Harii, *Germania* 43. 21, carried black shields. The escutcheons of the age of chivalry originated in this custom of the Germans. In the Roman army each cohort had its distinctive device or *digma* painted on its shields; on the column of Trajan at Rome such designs as a winged thunderbolt, a garland, and a laurel crown can be distinguished.

10. cassis aut galea: for the conventional distinction between these words, see lexicon. — **equi non . . . conspicui**: Caesar was forced to supply the German horsemen whom he requisitioned for service against Vercingetorix with new mounts, *quod minus idoneis equis utebantur*, *Bellum Gallicum* 7. 65. 4–5.

11. sed: agility in evolutions might have offset their natural defects, *but*, et seq. — **variare gyros**: *to execute changes of front in either direction;* such shifts were involved in describing the figure 8, a favorite maneuver in Roman equestrian drill. An essential difference between Roman and German methods of horsemanship is implied in the comment made in *Annales* 11. 16 on Italicus, a prince of the Cherusci, *ipse . . . armis equisque in patrium nostrumque morem exercitus* ('he . . . was trained in arms and in horsemanship after the mode of his country and in our fashion ').

12. uno flexu: *with a wheel constantly in one direction,* in contrast with *variare gyros*. — **dextros**: the language of Tacitus should not be so pressed as to lead to the inference that the German cavalry *could* not execute a left wheel but that they ordinarily *did* not. The point which Tacitus wished to emphasize is that the Germans were not trained to match the mobility which enabled a troop of Roman horsemen suddenly to shift from a turn in one direction into a turn in the other without breaking the alignment. In the case of a German column, a wheel begun in one direction was always completed. The right wheel alone is specified because it is the one which would more naturally occur to the mind as an example; furthermore, this evolution would be resorted to more commonly, since the side protected by the shield would be thus presented to the foe.

13. coniuncto orbe: not a very lucid expression, because it was actually the horsemen who were *coniuncti*, *orbe* being the circle or the arc of the circle of which the file of wheeling troops was the radius. Translate: *the wheeling file preserving its alignment*. — **in universum aestimanti**: the same phrase occurs in *Agricola* 11. 10.

14. plus ... roboris: cf. *Agricola* 12. 1, *in pedite robur; Germania* 30. 12, *omne robur (Chattorum) in pedite*. — **eoque**: = *ideoque*. The mode of fighting practiced by these combined forces is described in detail by Caesar, *Bellum Gallicum* 1. 48. We should infer from his account that each contingent contained an equal number of horse and foot, each cavalryman choosing his comrade from the infantry. The foot soldiers supported the horsemen in action and came to their rescue in case they were unhorsed. Caesar himself recognized the serviceability of such troops and utilized them in the war with Vercingetorix (cf. *Bellum Gallicum* 7. 65. 4–5) and in the Pharsalian campaign; cf. *Bellum Civile* 3. 75 and 84.

15. congruente ... velocitate: cf. *Bellum Gallicum* 1. 48. 7: *si quo erat longius prodeundum aut celerius recipiendum, tanta erat horum exercitatione celeritas, ut iubis sublevati equorum cursum adaequarent.*

16. ante aciem locant: not, of course, alone, but with their equestrian companions, whose presence in the same place follows as a matter of course.

17. numerus: i.e. *peditum delectorum*. As we should expect and as is illustrated by the passages from Caesar referred to above, the functions of the cavalry in combats in which the *mixti* were engaged, was taken for granted, hence in description is subordinated to the part played by the chosen infantry, the agility and prowess displayed by them. They were regarded as an élite body — thus in the Pharsalian campaign we find Caesar selecting them from the *antesignani* — and might well receive a distinctive name. — **pagis**: here a large territorial subdivision of a *civitas*, such as those into which the Suebi were divided according to Caesar, *Bellum Gallicum* 4. 1. The size of the Suebian *pagus* may be inferred from the fact that each was populous enough to put a thousand warriors in the field every year and to retain an equal number of men at home to till the fields.

19. acies: the main body of the army. — **per cuneos**: later writers liken this formation to a boar's head, *caput porcinum*.

20. cedere loco: the regular idiom for deserting one's post. Roman military theory disapproved even of strategic withdrawals; failure to maintain a prescribed position rendered soldiers liable to severe penalty, as the following passage in the *Life of Augustus*, written by Suetonius, a contemporary of Tacitus, well attests: ' If any cohorts gave way in battle (*si cessissent loco*), Augustus decimated them and fed the rest on barley (instead of the usual rations of wheat); when centurions left their posts, he punished them with death just as he did the rank and file' (chap. 24, Rolfe's translation).

21. quam: with ellipsis of *potius*, as in various passages elsewhere in the works of Tacitus.

22. praecipuum flagitium: *the height of infamy; praecipuus* has here a superlative,force, a frequent connotation of the word in Latin of this period. Cf. Montesquieu, *Spirit of the Laws* xxviii, chap. xxi: ' The ancient Salic Law allows a composition of fifteen sous (120 *denarii*) to any person that had been injuriously reproached with having left his buckler behind.' The severity of Spartan feeling toward the ῥίψασπις is well known; however, Greek poets and, after them, the Roman Horace were not above jesting on the subject.

23. concilium: the popular assembly described in chap. 11-12.

Chapter 7.

Military leaders, their choice and the extent of their powers; incentives to valor in battle.

1. reges: among the tribes of Germany supreme power was vested sometimes in one person, called by Tacitus the *rex*, sometimes in two or more *principes*. *Rex* and *principes* alike were scions of the family or families which, by virtue of ancient lineage, formed the top of the social structure of the tribe. Such preëminence was due ordinarily to a supposed divine origin. The king, where he existed, was that one of the *principes* in whose hands authority was centralized by popular choice. Eligibility only was hereditary; final option rested with the people.

As is shown by the case of the Cherusci, who, in the year 47 A.D. with the consent of the emperor Claudius, set up as king Italicus, the sole surviving member of the *regia stirps*, although in previous years they had been ruled by *principes*, monarchy and oligarchy might interchange in one tribe. However, in general the peoples of East Germany inclined to a single ruler, whereas in the West control was commonly in the hands of *principes*. — **ex** nobilitate : *on the ground of noble lineage.* — **duces:** called in Old High German *herzoga*, modern German, *Herzog*. Among tribes that had no king, the natural leader in war where he existed, a *dux* was chosen to exercise chief command; such tribal *duces* were Brinno among the Canninefates (*Historiae* 4. 15), Gannascus, chosen *dux* by the Chauci though himself a member of the Canninefates (*Annales* 11. 8). As in the cases of Ariovistus, Arminius, the conqueror of Varus, and Civilis, leader of the revolt of 69–70 A.D., a *dux* might head a confederation of several tribes. The selection of a *dux* was indicated by carrying him on an upraised shield, a ceremony which was perpetuated in the choice of a king among the later Goths and Franks. — **nec . infinita . . . potestas:** the German kings, owing as they did their position to popular choice, were inevitably limited in initiative and remained the instruments of the tribal will as expressed in the folk assembly.

2. exemplo: ablative of means, explained by the following clause.

4. admiratione: ablative of cause.

5. animadvertere: *to inflict capital punishment.* The Roman
general in the field had power of life and death over his men, an
authority symbolized by the attendant lictors and their fasces.
— **ne verberare quidem**: in conscious contrast with conditions in
the Roman army, where a flogging inflicted by the centurions was
a common punishment. In the mutiny of the Pannonian and
German legions (14 A.D.), the scourgings which they had suffered
formed one of the grievances of the malcontents: *Annales* 1. 17:
verbera et vulnera . . . sempiterna (' blows and wounds (were) con-
tinual '); 1. 35: *nudant universi corpora . . . verberum notas
exprobrant* (' all as one man bare their bodies . . . give voice to
reproaches because of the scars of floggings '). — **nisi sacerdotibus**: according to Caesar, *Bellum Gallicum* 6. 23. 4, command-
ers-in-chief did wield power of life and death. Caesar, influ-
enced by his familiarity with Roman practice, may have generalized on insufficient data, or, in the interval between Caesar and
Tacitus, conditions may have changed. Caesar's assertion,
Bellum Gallicum 6. 21. 1: *neque druides habent, qui rebus divinis
praesint, neque sacrificiis student,* in so far as it tends to minimize
the functions of the priest in German life, is also at variance with
the conditions portrayed by Tacitus, who, although he does not
imply the existence of a hierarchy comparable with the Druids,
assigns important prerogatives to the priest. The priest is the
authorized instrument of divine punishment, presides over
divination (chap. 10), has power to enforce silence in council
(chap. 11).

7. quem adesse . . credunt: besides Tiu and Wodan, the
chief war gods of German mythology, Donar, Freyr, and other
divinities were endowed with martial character and pictured as
participating in battles.

8. effigiesque et signa: in chap. 9 Tacitus says that the
Germans did not make statues portraying the gods in human
form. *Effigies* were images of animals symbolizing the gods and
sacred to them; thus the wolf was the animal of Wodan, the
boar of Freyr, the bear of Donar. The custom here referred to is
mentioned also in *Historiae* 4. 22: *depromptae silvis lucisque
ferarum imagines, ut cuique genti inire proelium mos est* (' effigies
of wild beasts were brought forth from forests and groves, accord-

ing to the custom of each tribe in entering battle ') ; *signa* were representations of the attributes of the several gods, such as the spear of Wodan, and the hammer of Donar. — **lucis**: the sacred groves mentioned in chap. 9 ; the eagles captured from the legions of Varus were kept in such precincts. Cf. *Annales* 1. 59: (*dixit*) *cerni adhuc Germanorum in lucis signa Romana, quae dis patriis suspenderit* (' he said that to the present day the Roman standards, which he had hung up in honor of (their) ancestral gods, were seen in the groves of the Germans').

11. turmam aut cuneum: the former a division of cavalry, the latter of infantry. — **familiae et propinquitates**: a military alignment based on kinship is the natural arrangement in a society in which family and clan retain their primitive places as distinct social and territorial units. In the *Iliad* 2. 362 f. Nestor commends the system to Agamemnon ; in comparatively modern times the Scotch fought by clans.

12. pignora: the women and children usually accompanied a barbarian army in the field ; cf. Caesar, *Bellum Gallicum* 1. 51 ; Tacitus, *Agricola* 38. 1 ; *Historiae* 4. 18 et al. — **audiri**: probably, if the text be correct, to be explained as an historical infinitive, although of the several instances in which Tacitus uses the construction in a subordinate clause, there is none in which it expresses customary action.

15. exigere: *to inspect*, not only with a view to employing curative measures, a function of the woman in primitive society, but also, as *numerare* suggests, to make sure that the warrior had acquitted himself with honor.

16. cibosque et hortamina: another example of a favorite stylistic turn ; cf. 1. 2, *metu aut montibus.*

Chapter 8.

The deference paid to woman.

2. obiectu pectorum: as a token that death at the hands of their own compatriots was to be preferred to falling into the power of the enemy. The behavior of the German women before the battle between Caesar and Ariovistus was actuated by the same motive: (*mulieres*) *ad proelium proficiscentes milites passis manibus flentes implorabant, ne se in servitutem*

Romanis traderent, Bellum Gallicum 1. 51. 3. The women of
the Cimbri, exhibiting a more desperate courage, killed the
fugitives before committing suicide themselves, Plutarch,
Marius 27.

3. comminus captivitate: join in translation — *the imminence
of captivity.* — **quam longe inpatientius . . . timent**: an unusual combination of words, since *inpatientius* is naturally
used of adversity borne *in praesenti* rather than dreaded *in
futuro.* Here both ideas are blended. Translate: *the terrors
of which they regard as far more unbearable on the women's account (than on their own).*

6. puellae quoque nobiles: *puellae* is the emphatic word; as a
rule, only persons of high rank were acceptable as hostages, hence
nobiles is, strictly speaking, dispensable. — **inesse**: sc. *feminis.*

7. providum: the Pythias, Sibyls, witches, and fortune-
tellers of many races and epochs prove that the tendency to
endow woman with mystic powers is universal. — **nec aut
consilia earum aspernantur**: recall Caesar's words, *Bellum
Gallicum* 1. 50. 4: *apud Germanos ea consuetudo (erat) ut matres
familiae eorum sortibus et vaticinationibus declararent, utrum
proelium committi ex usu esset necne.* In deference to the pro-
phetic advice of the women, Ariovistus refused to give battle
until the moon was full.

8. vidimus: the first person does not prove that Tacitus
saw Veleda with his own eyes; we know that she was taken
captive but not that she was actually brought to Rome. Tacitus
may well be expressing himself as spokesman for his time and
mean simply *nostra aetas vidit.*

9. Velĕdam: as we learn from several passages in the *Histories* in which mention of her is made, Veleda was an inspired
maiden of the tribe of the Bructeri. She lived apart in a tower
on the banks of the Lippe and, as a result of the prestige gained
by the fulfillment of her prophecies as to the success of German
arms, she shared with Civilis chief prominence in the revolt of
the Batavi in 69–70 A.D.

10. Albrūnam: not mentioned elsewhere. The name rests
on conjecture and means one ' endowed with the magic power
of the elves.'

11. nec tamquam facerent deas: on the surface this context expresses the fact that, in contrast with the simple reverence paid to prophetesses in earlier times, a later generation tended to exalt mystically endowed women into the standing of divinities; cf. *Veledam . . . numinis loco habitam* 1. 9 and also *Historiae* 4. 61. A Roman reader would inevitably see in the sentence a satirical thrust at the deification of the unfit among the women of the imperial houses, *e.g.* Poppaea Sabina, wife of Nero, and their daughter, who died in early infancy. Translate: *not in the thought that they were manufacturing goddesses;* there is a similar sarcastic touch in Horace, *Satires* 1. 8. 1–3:

> *Olim truncus eram ficulnus, inutile lignum,*
> *cum faber, incertus scamnum faceretne Priapum,*
> *maluit esse deum*

(' Once on a time I was the trunk of a fig tree, a useless log, when the craftsman, debating whether to fashion a settle or a Priapus, preferred that I should be a god '). Cf. Isaiah xliv. 15: " Yea, he kindleth it, and baketh bread; yea, he maketh a god and worshippeth it."

Observe the dexterous transition effected by the last clause in this chapter to the subject treated in the following chapter.

Chapter 9.

The chief divinities of the German pantheon.

1. deorum maxime Mercurium colunt: perhaps an echo of the sentence of Caesar, *Bellum Gallicum* 6. 17. 1, *deorum maxime Mercurium colunt*, in which, however, it is the chief divinity of the Gauls that is identified with Mercury. Caesar's assertion, *Bellum Gallicum* 6. 21. 2, that the Germans worshiped only the visible and beneficent phenomena of nature, such as the Sun, Moon, and Fire, and knew nothing of other gods, is widely at variance with the account of Tacitus and is based on insufficient knowledge. Worship of the powers of nature, universal among Indo-Europeans at one time, undoubtedly survived to some extent among the Germans of the first century B.C.; vestiges of sun worship are most readily traceable. Nevertheless, even at that period, anthropomorphic cults, such as those mentioned in this chapter, had quite overshadowed nature worship.

Mercurius is the Roman analogue of Wodan, partial correspondence in attributes and functions sufficing, as is usual in instances of this sort, to establish identification. Thus the *petasus* and the *caduceus* of Mercury were comparable to the broad-brimmed hat and the magic wand of Wodan. Wodan was the god of death; the Greek Hermes was a *psychopompus* or conductor of souls to the other world. Each god presided over trade and commerce. The question is debatable as to which of these analogies especially contributed to the identification, clear evidence of which still survives in the correspondence of English *Wednesday*, derived from the *Wodanstag* of certain German tribes, with the French *Mercredi* (*dies Mercurii*).

Tacitus writes as though Wodan were the chief divinity of the whole German race. As a matter of fact, his cult had no such universal currency; his worship flourished especially among the peoples who dwelt near the Rhine and Tacitus generalized from this fact. — certis diebus: *at stated festivals.*

2. humanis quoque hostiis: the custom of human sacrifice, characteristic of the lower stages of religious development and surviving even in more enlightened epochs, was by no means so restricted among the Germans as the words of Tacitus in this passage would indicate. Wodan, as the god of death, was a favored recipient of human victims offered as a prophylactic measure by those whose lives were, or might be, in jeopardy. However, in his case the practice was not limited to fixed occasions, and, furthermore, it was a feature of other cults, *e.g.* that of the sovereign god of the Suebi, that of Nerthus (cf. chap. 39 and 40), and of Tiu, the war god; cf. *Annales* 13. 57, where it is related that the Hermunduri immolated the defeated army of the Chatti to Tiu and Wodan. Human sacrifice was resorted to also in times of famine and to avert the perils of the sea; instances of the persistence of the rite among Teutonic races are found throughout the first ten centuries of our era and even beyond. — **Herculem**: *i.e.* Donar; cf. note on chap. 3. 1.

3. Martem: *i.e.* Tiu, originally the lord of the heavens, akin to Zeus and Jupiter, and chief of all the gods; he gradually developed into the war god *par excellence* of the Germans, hence his identification in the *interpretatio Romana* with Mars, proof of which appears in the translation of *dies Martis*, French *Mardi*, into the old Germanic originals of *Dienstag, Tuesday.* The divine province of Tiu underwent some modification as the result of the extension among certain races of the functions of Wodan, who displaced Tiu to a certain extent from supremacy in the pantheon. As a death god Wodan also tended more and more, especially among the Scandinavian peoples, to usurp a place as a god of war. — **concessis animalibus:** *with victims which are permissible;* written from the point of view of Roman religion which, in the age of Tacitus, would regard human victims as *incastae.*

4. Isidi: it is impossible to establish the definite Germanic counterpart. Evidently the connection of a sacred ship or a shiplike symbol with the cult ritual of some Teutonic goddess, suggested to Tacitus or his source the so-called Navigium Isidis; in the course of this festival, celebrated March 5, a vessel laden with spices, and consecrated to Isis, was launched on the sea. This rite commemorated the advent of spring and the opening of navigation. It is possible, but not certain, that it was a native goddess of productivity to whom the name Isis is here applied.

5. nisi quod: introducing a qualification of the preceding statement as in *Agricola* 6. 5. — **signum ipsum:** *the very emblem.* — **liburnae:** see on *Agricola* 28. 5. It is not the type of the ship as such that impels Tacitus to regard the cult as an importation, but simply the fact that the symbol is a ship.

6. religionem: do not render by the English derivative. — **ceterum:** indicating a return to the topic of the native religion after the digression concerning a divinity assumed to be an importation.

This sentence reflects a tendency, frequently discernible in this treatise, to exalt German ideals and life above Roman. Tacitus here ascribes to the Germans of his time a degree of spiritual refinement and philosophical insight quite beyond them.

7. nec cohibere parietibus: groves, stone cairns, and precincts fenced in by stones but open to the sky, constituted the
Germans' sanctuaries, to which, however, the word *templum* in
its literal sense of ' sacred inclosure,' may be applied; cf. chap.
40. 16, where it is a synonym for *nemus*. The statement of
Tacitus as to the non-existence of temples is confirmed by the
archaeological evidence, but his explanation of the fact is erroneous. The absence of temple structures was due not to
philosophical conviction but to the primitive stage of religious
development reached by the Germans. A striking parallel
to this passage is the account of the nature-worshiping Persians,
found in Herodotus 1. 131: ' The Persians, I am aware, observe
usages of this sort, not deeming it lawful to set up statues,
temples, and shrines; but they impute folly to such as do these
things, according to my way of thinking, because they do not
believe, as do the Greeks, that the gods have human forms.' —
in ullam humani oris speciem: a few specimens of wooden
idols, fashioned into a rude semblance of the human form,
have been unearthed in Teutonic lands, notably in Denmark.
At present the data do not suffice to show that such anthropomorphic representations of gods had developed independently
among the Germans in prehistoric times; they may well be
due to Roman influence. Hence the assertion of Tacitus may
stand, especially in view of the fact that, as appears from the
context, he had in mind chiefly the temple statues of the Roman
gods, with which, of course, there was nothing strictly comparable among the Germans.

8. ex: *in keeping with.*

9. lucos ac nemora: " the groves were God's first temples "
(Bryant, *A Forest Hymn*). Mention of sacred groves is not
infrequent in Tacitus; thus, chap. 39. 3–4, *in silvam . . .
sacram;* 40. 8–9, the *castum nemus* of Nerthus; *Annales* 2. 12,
in silvam Herculi sacram.

10. secretum illud: *that mysterious entity.* Compare with
the spirit of this context the words of Tacitus as to the Jews,
Historiae 5. 5: *Iudaei mente sola unumque numen intellegunt; pro-
fanos qui deum imagines mortalibus materiis in species hominum
effingant* (' the Jews believe in one god, comprehensible to

E

the mind alone; they regard as impious those who fashion idols out of perishable material into the forms of human beings ').

Chapter 10.

Methods of divination.

1. auspicia sortesque: the former is the broader term and includes the several methods of divination mentioned in the chapter exclusive of the lot. Recall Caesar, *Bellum Gallicum* 1. 50. 4 (quoted in note on 8. 7), where we are told that the German matrons resorted to the lot in order to discover the propitious time for battle; also 1. 53. 7, in which it is narrated that the Germans had recourse to the lots three times to determine the fate of Valerius Procillus, a friend of Caesar held captive by Ariovistus. — **ut qui maxime**: elliptical for *ut ii qui maxime observant.* — **sortium**: divination by lot was so wide- spread as to amount to a folk custom in antiquity. The prac- tice existed among peoples so far separated as Scythians, Celts, Italians, Finns, and Teutons. Among the Italians Caere, Falerii, and Patavium were centers of the process and the *sortes* of the temple of Fortune at Praeneste were especially famous. Cicero, *De Divinatione* 2. 41. 85–87, flouts the method as a tissue of fraud; nevertheless the *sortilegus* continued to be a feature of the life of Augustan and imperial Rome; cf. Horace, *Satires* 1. 9. 29 f.; Tibullus, 1. 3. 11–12; Juvenal, 6. 583; Apuleius, *Metamorphoses* 9. 8.

2. simplex: *uniform.* — **virgam**: wood, since it was most readily obtainable and easily incised, was the material most used for the *sortes* among primitive peoples. In Italy as well, the wooden lot seems to have been the sanctioned type in gen- eral: Plautus, *Casina* 384, refers to those made of poplar or fir wood; the lots used at Praeneste were made of oak; cf. Cicero's description, *De Divinatione* 2. 41. 85: *declarant perfracto saxo sortis erupisse in robore insculptas priscarum litterarum notis* (' they assert . . . that, when the rock had been cleft, there burst from it lots composed of the characters of an archaic alphabet incised on oak wood '). However, interesting specimens of bronze *sortes* have been found; see the *Corpus Inscriptionum Latinarum*, vol. 1, nos. 1438 et seq. — **frugiferae arbori**: not a fruit tree in our sense of the term. *Frugifer* is applied to any tree or shrub which produces nuts or berries, *e.g.* the oak, beech, elder, and juniper. The prerequisite here mentioned was not observed universally by all peoples who resorted to divination of this mode. Thus the Finns took no cognizance of such a rule; the Scythians used willow wands (Herodotus, 4. 67); see also the reference in Plautus mentioned above.

3. notis: signs or symbols, carrying with them some definite implication and, as the following sentence shows, widely intelligible, since the father of the household was able to interpret them as well as the priest. Some scholars have preferred to see in these *notae* a reference to the characters of the Runic alphabet, derived from the Latin capitals. However it is doubtful whether the Runes were known to the Germans in the first century A.D. In any case, so strong is the conservative tendency in matters pertaining to religion and the occult, that the traditional signs would have maintained themselves for a time in the face of an innovation. The prestige of the lots of Praeneste rested partly on the fact that they were written in an archaic alphabet; cf. Cicero, *De Divinatione* 2. 41. 85, quoted above.

5. publice: *as an affair of state.*

6. pater familiae: as was the case in Roman religion, the father officiated as family priest in the ceremonies of the household ritual. It is noteworthy that, in contrast with Caesar, *Bellum Gallicum* 1. 50. 4, Tacitus ignores the *matres familiae* as diviners by lot. In Roman usage procedure varied. Often, owing to the common folk belief that the guilelessness of childhood commended it especially as the vehicle for expressing the divine purposes, a *puer* played an important part in the ceremony; at Praeneste he shuffled and drew the lots; sometimes he seems to have acted as interpreter; cf. Tibullus, 1. 3. 11–12. In Horace's parody of the practice, a Sabine crone acts as *sortilegus; Satires* 1. 9. 29 f. — **caelumque suspiciens**: not to avoid seeing the *surculi* but as an expression of a petition for divine guidance to be disclosed in the lots.

7. ter singulos: a choice was made three times and each time one was " raised," as the operation was technically termed. *Numero deus impare gaudet*, says Vergil, *Eclogues* 8. 75; the number three has been especially favored in ritual and ceremony among all peoples from early times down to the present. Besides the present passage, Herodotus, 4. 67, Caesar, *Bellum Gallicum* 1. 53. 7, and Tibullus, 1. 3. 11–12, bear witness to its significance in divination by lot. — **impressam**: *incised*. English *write*, akin to German *einritzen*, testifies to the fact that incision was the primitive method of chirography.

10. adhuc: *besides*. In Roman practice as well, results obtained by one method of divination might be subjected to further test; thus in Pliny, *Letters* 2. 20, the legacy hunter Regulus, after assuring his dupe, Verania, that her horoscope portends recovery from her illness, resorts to an haruspex to confirm the prophecy of the stars. — **quidem**: implying, as usual, a contrast, which in this case is contained in *proprium . . experiri* following. — **hic**: *apud Germanos*. As in chap. 3. 10, *hunc Oceanum*, the reader is transported in thought to Germany.

11. proprium: *the characteristic (method of divination).* Among the Persians also, the actions of horses were regarded as constituting omens; hence it was, according to Herodotus, 3. 84, that, prior to the accession of Darius to the throne, it was agreed among the rival claimants that he whose horse should first neigh at sunrise should reign.

13. isdem   lucis: the sacred groves referred to in chap. 9. — **candidi**: the canonical color for sacred animals and those of celestial breed; recall the white bull of Europa, the white steeds of Castor and Pollux, to say nothing of the white elephant of Siam! Sacred white horses accompanied the Persian armies; cf. Herodotus, 1. 189; 7. 40.

14. pressos: actually, of course, by the yoke of the chariot.

15. rex vel princeps: according to whether the government of the state was monarchical or oligarchical. — **comitantur**: to be understood literally; they escorted the sacred chariot on foot. So in the army of Xerxes the eight white horses which drew the chariot of Ahuramazda were driven by a charioteer who followed on foot because no mortal was allowed to mount to the car; cf. the similar procedure in the case of the *vehiculum* of Nerthus, chap. 40. 10 f.

16. fremitus: (*other*) *sounds*, such as stampings and snortings.

17. apud sacerdotes: faith in these oracles was not restricted to the credulous populace but was shared by the upper classes, who, as judged by the attitude of their Roman compeers in these matters, might have been expected to hold skeptical views concerning the infallibility of auspices and to have manipulated them to suit their own ends.

18. putant: supply *proceres et sacerdotes*.

22. committunt: a technical " sporting " formula from the language of the arena: cf. Juvenal, 1. 162:

> *securus licet Aenean Rutulumque ferocem*
> *committas*, et seq.

(' you may without concern match Aeneas and the doughty Rutulian '). Except in Suetonius *componere* is the commoner term. Such combats of chosen champions were ordinarily resorted to to effect a final settlement of an issue, *e.g.* in the story of the Horatii and the Curiatii (Livy, 1. 24 f.), in the dispute between the Argives and the Spartans for the possession of Thyreatis (Herodotus, 1. 82), and in the " judgment of God," a custom of the age of chivalry familiar to readers of Ivanhoe.

Chapter 11.

The popular assembly.

1. principes: as in 5. 12, used in the broad sense of *leading men*. In monarchical states the king shared in the deliberations of the *principes*, who probably formed a standing council or senate. — consultant: they deliberated, as we say, " with power."

2. omnes: in the popular assembly or *Thing*, comprising all men of free birth, both the commons and the *principes*, and in this respect comparable to the ἀγορή of the Homeric Greeks.

3. pertractentur: the results reached after careful deliberation by the *principes* were presented as reports to the assembly, to be accepted or rejected.

4. certis: *regularly appointed.* Regular sessions were held only at the time of the new or the full moon, not at every such period, but two or three times a year.

6. auspicatissimum initium: on the advice of the prophetesses, Ariovistus avoided battle until the time of the full moon, Caesar, *Bellum Gallicum* 1. 50; the Spartans refused to march to the aid of the Athenians at Marathon until the moon was at its full, Herodotus, 6. 106.

7. numerum . . . noctium computant: a procedure which logically accompanied the computation of time according to the moon's phases. The Gauls also calculated time in terms of nights; cf. Caesar, *Bellum Gallicum* 6. 18. Our English *fortnight* and *twelfthnight* are survivals of this practice of our Teutonic forefathers. — **constituunt . . . condicunt:** supply *diem; they set a day and agree upon it.*

8. nox ducere diem videtur: cf. the language of Caesar, *Bellum Gallicum* 6. 18. 2: *Galli   et mensium et annorum initia sic observant ut noctem dies subsequatur.* The same conception, which still holds good among the Jews and the Mohammedans, reveals itself in the marked preference in the Homeric poems for the word order νύκτας τε καὶ ἤματα.

9. nec ut iussi: *not like persons acting in response to a command.* The penchant for individual freedom of action exhibited by the Germans was bound to provoke comment on the part of a Roman, since his prejudice was all in favor of carefully ordered parliamentary procedure and punctilious coöperation; cf. *Historiae* 4. 76: *(dixit) Germanos . . non iuberi, non regi,* sed cuncta ex libidine agere ('he said that the Germans . . . were not subject to orders or control, but acted in all things according to their fancy'). Throughout this account of the German assembly, the contrasts with Roman usage are present in the mind of the writer.

11. ut turbae placuit: the formal call to order waited on the convenience of the throng, an ultra-democratic arrangement. — **armati:** cf. chap. 13. 1. The attitude of the Roman toward this practice, so essentially at variance with his own, but characteristic of a stage of civilization in which military organization is the basis of civic life, is well illustrated by Livy,

21. 20, who refers (as does Caesar, *Bellum Gallicum* 5. 56. 1) to the *armatum concilium* of the Gauls: *in iis nova terribilisque species visa est, quod armati — ita mos gentis erat — in concilium venerunt.*

12. per sacerdotes: as representatives of the gods, in whose name a sacred truce, observed during the session, was proclaimed. In Homeric times the officials who convened the assembly were not the priests but the heralds, who were, however, sacrosanct as being under the protection of Zeus; hence their epithets θεῖοι, ' divine,' and Διὶ φίλοι, ' dear to Zeus.' — et **coercendi**: a breach of the peace would be an offense against the gods, for whom the priests would act as deputies in inflicting punishment, precisely as in the case of infractions of military discipline; cf. chap. 7. 7: *velut deo imperante.* Upon the Homeric herald also devolved the task of keeping order in the assembly and quelling disputants; cf. *Iliad* 7. 274.

13. rex vel princeps: as in 10. 15, the expression is adapted to cover assemblies of either monarchical or non-monarchical states. — **prout . . . audiuntur**: the Roman reader would be impressed with the contrast here presented with the procedure followed in the senate, the sole Roman legislative body at this time. In the senate, *ius sententiae dicendae* was controlled solely by official position, *i.e.* membership in the body of the *consulares, praetorii,* et cet., within these classes by seniority, and was not subject to variation in favor of such elements of personal prestige as *decus bellorum, facundia.*

16. concutiunt: *they clash one upon the other.* The Gauls employed this method of applause under similar circumstances; cf. Caesar, *Bellum Gallicum* 7. 21. 1.

Chapter 12.

The judiciary; the penal code.

1. accusare quoque: the assembly was not only a deliberative body but could also legally exercise judicial functions. — **discrimen capitis intendere**: *to lay a charge involving capital punishment.*

3. arboribus suspendunt: among the Greeks and the Romans hanging was resorted to as a means of suicide; strangulation, however, the nearest approach to hanging, had a recognized place in the Roman penal code. — **ignavos et imbelles**: these words are paired also in *Agricola* 15. 11 and in *Germania* 31. 7.

4. corpore infames: *morally degenerate.* — **caeno ac palude**: combine in translating.

5. crate mergunt: Livy, 1. 51, describes an isolated instance of the infliction of this penalty in the time of Tarquinius Superbus: *ut novo genere leti deiectus (Turnus) . . . crate superne iniecta saxisque congestis mergeretur.* Among the ancient and the medieval Germans this mode of execution was reserved primarily for female offenders; hence its employment in the case of male culprits branded their transgressions as especially unmanly.

6. tamquam: here, as frequently in Tacitus, introducing the motive which is present in the mind of the agent and controls his action. — **scelera** . **flagitia**: *crimes* and *abominations:* the former looks toward the victim, the latter has primary reference to the personal infamy incurred by the sinner.

7. levioribus delictis: among these was homicide; cf. chap. 21. 3. — **pro modo poena**: a Roman reader would not see in the allusions contained in this chapter to the Germanic method of graduating punishments according to the magnitude of the offense, a superfluous stressing of the only justifiable procedure. Though in practice the Roman method did not differ in this respect from the German, yet a cardinal doctrine of Stoicism, the regnant school of thought in the time of Tacitus, was that in theory all offenses were equal; see, *e.g.*, Cicero, *Academica* 2. 43. 133: *placet Stoicis omnia peccata esse paria.* Horace, *Satires* 1. 3. 96 f., ridicules this tenet as repugnant to reason and unworkable in practice, and recommends: *adsit | Regula peccatis quae poenas inroget aequas.*

8. equorum pecorumque numero: live stock, being the chief source of wealth, was the natural legal tender. From the usage here described, developed in later Germanic laws the elaborate system of regulating the compounding of crimes and felonies on the basis of pecuniary compensation, known as *Wergeld.* Fines were adjusted " to fit the crime."

9. regi vel civitati: this procedure was based on the theory that the perpetrator of a crime had sinned against the state as well as against the victim. Hence in monarchical states the king, elsewhere the community, received as compensation for the breach of public peace which had been committed, a percentage of the *Wergeld*.

10. propinquis eius: when murder had been done or when for some other cause the injured party had not lived to receive his compensation. — **eliguntur . . . et principes**: the judicial administration of the cantons was in the hands of certain qualified members of the existing body of *principes;* selection of the *principes* to be intrusted with this function was another prerogative of the tribal assembly. These officials were perhaps the *principes regionum* mentioned by Caesar, *Bellum Gallicum* 6. 23. 5: *in pace nullus est communis magistratus sed principes regionum atque pagorum inter suos ius dicunt controversiasque minuunt.*

11. per pagos vicosque: the *pagi* were extensive subdivisions of the *civitas;* see note on 6. 17; each formed a judicial district throughout which the presiding *princeps* held court in circuit. The addition of *vicos* simply characterizes in a general way the *pagus* as an aggregation of village communities; in certain of them the sittings were held. — **iura . reddunt**: this formula and Caesar's *ius dicere* (see note 10 above) give in Roman legal phraseology the technical definition of the activity of the praetors, with whom, however, the judicial *principes* were analogous only in their capacity of presiding justices. Verdicts were dependent on the *consilium,* ' advice,' and *auctoritas,* ' sanction,' of the hundred assessors, representing the people of a *pagus.* The *princeps* was responsible for the announcement and the execution of the collective decision. — **centeni**: in later times called *Hunnones.* When Tacitus was describing this judicial institution of the Germans, he must have compared it in thought with the *centumviri* or ' court of the hundred men,' of which we read so frequently in the *Letters* of Pliny. This name was an approximation to the number, since there were at first 105 members, and was retained after the chamber was increased to 180. Similarly, in later times, assistants at German courts were called *Hunnones*, when the name had ceased to have any numerical significance.

Chapter 13.

The investiture with arms; the *comitatus*.

1. nihil . . . nisi armati agunt: Thucydides, 1. 6, tells how in early times in Greece men lived always under arms, ' as do barbarians.'

2. moris: a characteristic usage; cf. *Agricola* 33. 1 and 42. 20.

3. suffecturum probaverit: *has passed favorably on his competence.*

4. principum aliquis: the ceremony of investiture would normally be performed by the father if he were alive; however, one of the chiefs, on whose favor the novitiate had a claim, might act *in loco parentis* for the reasons mentioned below.

5. apud illos toga: being the German counterpart of the assumption of the *toga virilis*.

6. pars . . . rei publicae: inasmuch as he thereafter participated in the privileges and the duties of citizenship; the sentence does not imply that there was a complete breaking of home ties and emancipation from the *patria potestas*.

7. insignis nobilitas aut . . merita: or both, since the two attributes are not mutually exclusive. — **principis dignationem**: *condescension on the part of a chief, i.e.* investiture with arms at his hands.

8. etiam adulescentulis: those below the period of *iuventa*, the normal age for military service. — **adsignant**: *entitle to.*

9. robustioribus: the mature and seasoned members of the following but who may not possess inherited claim to distinction. — **adgregantur**: *they align themselves with.* — **nec rubor . . . adspici**: they are not ashamed to waive their inherited claims to priority and take a place in the ranks, as it were, of the following.

10. quin etiam: *what is more;* herewith is expressed a further possible qualification of the standing of the young noble in the following; he not only takes a place among his fellows as one among many, but he is liable to see others on the score of merit and experience enjoy a higher position in the esteem of the *princeps* than does he. — **comitatus**: in this institution is the origin of feudal vassalage — the group of henchmen paying fealty to a chief, his followers in war and his table companions in peace.

13. locus: supply *sit*.

15. decus . . . praesidium: these words are also joined in one context in the famous lines which begin Horace, *Odes* 1. 1:

> *Maecenas atavis edite regibus,*
> *O et praesidium et dulce decus meum.*

17. comitatus: preferably taken as a genitive.

19. profligant: *they all but finish*. It is unnecessary to take this word in a sense other than that most frequent in Livy and Tacitus, where it commonly implies virtual, not total, completion in contrast with *conficere;* cf. Livy, 21. 40. 11: *bellum commissum ac profligatum conficere.* Tacitus means that the terror of the name of a famous *comitatus* often decides the issue of a war, which, however, is not ended until they actually engage in the conflict.

Chapter 14.

The *comitatus* in war.

2. iam vero: *moreover;* a transition to a stronger statement as in *Agricola* 9. 8; 21. 6.

3. superstitem . recessisse: among other examples of the loyalty of the *comites* to their chief, we are told by Ammianus Marcellinus, a historian of the fourth century A.D., that the two hundred *comites* of Chnodomar, king of the Alamanni, voluntarily surrendered themselves when he had been defeated and captured at the battle of Strassburg in 357 A.D.; *Ammianus Marcellinus* 16. 12. 60. As an illustration of similar personal devotion, though from another field, we may recall that when Cyrus the Younger died, his friends and table companions fell fighting in his defense with the exception of Ariaeus; Xenophon, *Anabasis* 1. 9. 31.

5. sua . . . facta gloriae eius adsignare: mentioned in *Agricola* 8. 9–11 as a worthy act of a dutiful subordinate. — **praecipuum sacramentum**: the *comites* are represented as

binding themselves by an oath of service analogous to that
sworn in allegiance to the emperor by the Roman soldiers and
renewed yearly. Vegetius, a writer of the early fifth century A.D., quotes this oath as follows: *iurant autem milites,
omnia prae se strenue facturos quae praeceperit imperator, numquam deserturos, nec mortem recusaturos pro Romana republica*
(' the soldiers take oath that they will discharge to the best of
their ability the commands of the general, will never desert
their post, will never refuse to die in defense of the Roman
state '); *De Re Militari* 2. 5.

10. inter ancipitia: *amid the hazards* (of warfare).

12. liberalitate: a departure, typical of our author and other
writers of the Empire, from the strict usage of classical prose,
according to which a prepositional phrase would be the normal
construction. — bellatorem: the use of verbal substantives as
adjectives is not uncommon in Latin of all periods, especially
with nouns in *-tor* and their feminines, and occurs with other
nouns as well; cf. Catullus, 68. 46, *anus charta;* Livy, 1. 34. 5,
Lucumonem exsule advena ortum.

13. nam: giving the reason why their demands on the gener-
osity of the chief are thus limited; a preceding sentence *stipen-
dium non exigunt* is implied.

14. epulae   apparatus: the former word has reference
to the feast itself; the latter to the various ingredients and
concomitants, which among the Romans would include not
only food and drink but garlands and perfumes; cf. Horace,
Odes 1. 38, *Persicos odi, puer, apparatus*, et seq. Such refinements, of course, were lacking to German banquets, hence
incompti.

16. annum: = *annonam*, as in *Agricola* 31. 5.

17. vocare: = *provocare.* The thought of this passage,
which, although it applies to the *comites*, is nevertheless colored
by the typical Roman conception of the Germans, is paralleled
by the ideals of life attributed by Herodotus, 5. 6, to the Thracians: ' It is deemed that the idler is the most honorable, the
tiller of the soil the least honorable; that a livelihood gained
from war and pillage is the best.' ·

18. sudore adquirere . . . sanguine parare: the chapter

closes in the Tacitean manner, with an effective sentence —
note the antithesis, heightened by alliteration.

Chapter 15.

The *comitatus* in time of peace.

1. ineunt: the subject is the *princeps* and the *comites*. The
comitatus is still uppermost in the mind of the writer, as the
allusion to *principes* in line 8 shows. — **non multum venatibus**
on the surface a restriction of Caesar's testimony as to the
devotion to the chase characteristic of the Germans; cf. *Bellum
Gallicum* 4. 1. 8 : *multumque sunt in venationibus (Suebi)* ; 6. 21. 3 :
vita omnis in venationibus atque in studiis rei militaris consistit.
However, Caesar is speaking of a universal racial trait; Tacitus
is thinking primarily of a privileged warrior class.

3. nihil agens: explained by the following ablative absolute
construction. — **domus et penatium**: *penatium cura* has reference to the more intimate concerns of the household. The
combination *domus et penatium* bears much the same connotation as our " house and home."

5. familia : here in the restricted sense of the English derivative.

6. ament inertiam et oderint quietem : an oxymoron based
on the double meaning of *quies*, which, like English *repose*, may
mean either rest or slumber — *they love indolence and hate repose (of peace).*

7. viritim : the gifts were bestowed on the *princeps* by individuals directly, not by the state as a whole. In later times
these voluntary donations passed into a compulsory tax.

8. armentorum : such a partitive genitive, following a verb
" whose action affects the object only in part," is a frequent
construction in Greek.

11. magna arma : in chap. 6 we are told that, owing to the
comparative scarcity of iron, swords were rare among the Germans, comparatively speaking, and that the *framea* had only
a short point. Hence large weapons, involving as they would
a more lavish expenditure of iron for blade and point respectively,
would be held at a premium.

12. phalerae : medallions, used as trappings for horses and
worn as articles of personal adornment. Specimens have been

found in ancient graves in Germany. — **torques**: metal rings, worn as armlets or collars. These, as well as *phalerae*, were decorations bestowed on Roman soldiers as rewards for bravery. — **pecuniam accipere docuimus**: bribery of native chieftains had on more than one occasion served Rome as an effective device in her dealings with her northern foemen. Transactions of this kind, carried on by Domitian with Chariomerus, king of the Cherusci and Decebalus, king of the Dacians, were still fresh in the public memory when Tacitus was writing the *Germania;* cf. also chap. 42. 10 and *Historiae* 4. 76: *pecuniam ac dona, quis solis corrumpantur (Germani)* ('money and gifts, the sole means by which the Germans are corrupted ').

Chapter 16.

Habitations and houses.

1. nullas urbes: walled towns of some size, such as had been from time immemorial the civic centers typical of Greek and Roman life. We hear of *oppida* among the Germans, but these, though fortified, were not intended as places of permanent residence; like the stockades of pioneer times in this country, they were places of refuge in time of war. The Roman regarded the founding of walled towns as marking a milestone in human progress; cf. Lucretius, *De Rerum Natura* 5. 1108:

> *condere coeperunt urbis arcemque locare*
> *praesidium reges ipsi sibi perfugiumque*

('kings began to found cities and to lay out a citadel as a buttress to their power and a place of refuge '), echoed by Horace, *Satires* 1. 3. 104–105:

> *. . . dehinc absistere bello,*
> *oppida coeperunt munire et ponere leges*

(' then they began to cease from war, to fortify towns, and to enact laws '). On isolation of residence as an attribute of barbarism, see *Agricola* 21. 2.

2. sedes: it has been assumed ordinarily that this word means *dwellings*, hence that this clause merely anticipates the thought of the context *vicos locant*, et cet. A recent and plausible explanation takes the word in the common sense of *tribal seat* or *domain;* the reference will then be to the racial desire for isolation mentioned by Caesar, *Bellum Gallicum* 4. 3. 1 and 6. 23. 1, which impelled each stock to seek to maintain a zone of deserted land about its country. Take *inter se* with *iunctas.* — discreti ac diversi: these words refer to the dispersion of the village communities throughout the country and to their unmethodical arrangement in respect to communication with one another.

3. ut fons . . placuit: hence the frequency to this day in Germany of names of towns ending in *-brunn, -bach, -wald,* and occasionally in *-feld.*

4. conexis et cohaerentibus aedificiis: as in the " blocks " in our larger cities, and in the cities and towns generally in Europe.

5. spatio: a *court* or *yard.* English *yard,* German *Garten,* Latin *hortus,* and Greek χόρτος are all traceable to an Indo-Germanic base *gharta,* ' a place surrounded.'

6. adversus casus ignis remedium: a suggestion based on familiarity with Roman fire ordinances. A regulation in the *Laws of the Twelve Tables* provides for a space of 5 feet between the outer walls of adjacent buildings. However the statute had evidently become a dead letter before the time of Tacitus. After the fire of Nero, one of the precautions taken to provide against the repetition of the calamity was the prohibition of single partition walls; see *Annales* 15. 43.

The wooden houses of the Germans were, of course, easily combustible, but the explanation of the practice is to be sought, at least partly, in the racial insistence on the domestic independence of the individual. The saying " An Englishman's home is his castle " illustrates the persistence of this spirit among Anglo-Saxons.

8. materia: *timber.* — informi: *rough-hewn.* In a primitive type of German house, not mentioned by Tacitus, the walls were composed of a kind of basketry, which was covered with clay. — citra: *lacking;* on this Tacitean use of *citra* instead of *sine,* see *Agricola* 1. 12.

10. pura: *free from foreign substances,* hence it could be applied in a smooth coat. — ut . . . imitetur: *so that it gives the impression of painting and patterns in color.*

11. subterraneos specus: utilized by various races in antiquity for different purposes. Xenophon and his army encountered them in Armenia, where they served at once as stables, store-rooms, and places of abode. Similar chambers have been found in modern times in these regions; see H. F. Tozer, *Turkish Armenia*, p. 396. Vergil, *Georgics* 3. 376, describes the peoples of the frozen North as taking their ease *in defossis specubus . . . sub alta . . . terra.* Underground rooms were used for spinning by German women, ancient and medieval.

12. receptaculum frugibus: cf. Xenophon, *Anabasis* 4. 5. 25: ' In these underground dwellings were wheat, barley, pulse, and barley wine in bowls.'

15. fallunt: *escape detection.*

Chapter 17.

Clothing.

1. tegumen omnibus: the distinctive national dress, worn by all classes, was comparable to the Roman *sagum*, a short woolen mantle, fastened only at the neck and worn especially by soldiers and laborers. Caesar, *Bellum Gallicum* 6. 21. 5, describes the Germans as clothed in skins or furs. — **fibula**: many specimens, made of various metals and representing periods of technique extending from the early bronze age to Roman times, have been found in graves. For the various types see F. Kauffmann, *Deutsche Altertumskunde*, vol. 1 (Munich, 1913), Plates 14, 22, 25, and 32.

2. cetera: *otherwise;* this applies only to the garb worn in the house. — **totos dies   agunt**: some editors take *ago* in its common intransitive sense, equal to *vivere*, and explain *dies* as an accusative of duration. However, such passages as *Dialogus* 7, *non diem laetiorem egi*, *Historiae* 3. 38, *quod . . . laetos dies ageret*, and *Historiae* 2. 49, *noctem quietam   . egit*, strongly support the alternative view.

3. locupletissimi veste distinguuntur: *veste* is the keyword of the sentence. The obvious implication is that *vestis, i.e.* underwear, consisting of tunic and leggings, of woven material, was worn only by the very rich. Common sense, however, would forbid us to infer that the *sagum* was the sole out-door apparel of the masses, at least in severe weather. Even a primitive people suits its costume to the climate. Those Germans who could not afford or obtain cloth, substituted skins, and since this undoubtedly included the majority of the population, Caesar's generalization, referred to above, had some justification. — **non fluitante**: referring not so much to the flowing garments in general characteristic of Oriental garb as to the loose trousers, *anaxyrides*, which, in the eyes of the Greeks and the Romans, formed the outstanding feature of the costume of the Eastern peoples.

5. gerunt: sc. *Germani*.

6. neglegenter . . . exquisitius: among the peoples who dwelt near the Rhine and the Danube and had become familiar with civilized garb, skins were no longer highly esteemed as articles of apparel, hence those who wore them were careless in their choice. Tribes that lived apart from the zone of Roman influence and trade were discriminating.

7. cultus: *finery.* — **velamina**: a poetic word, chosen not only because of our author's partiality for novel locutions but also because it can be applied alike to the skins and to the garments made from them. Our English word " vestures " might suggest the stylistic effect.

8. spargunt: Vergil, *Eclogues* 2. 41, writes of the dappled roe *capreoli sparsis etiam nunc pellibus albo* (' roes with their skins even now dappled with white '). — **maculis pellibusque**: hendiadys for *maculis pellium*. Pieces cut from the skins of animals not native to Germany were attached to the original pelt; being different from it in color, these patches are called *maculae*. — **beluarum**: we may conjecture that seals were among the animals here alluded to; the ideas of Tacitus as to the genus and species of his *beluae* were probably vague enough.

9. Oceanus atque ignotum mare: as in chap. 2. 4 f., *adversus Oceanus . . . praeter periculum . . . ignoti maris*, the far reaches of the mysterious Northern Ocean, the *mare pigrum et grave* of *Agricola* 10. 20, are doubtless meant. — **nec alius feminis quam viris habitus**: this is also true of the Eskimo.

10. saepius: *rather frequently.* — **lineis amictibus**: taking the place of the woolen *sagum* as outer garment.

F

11. purpura : a red border or stripe.

12. vestitus : like *vestis* above, *the undergarment.* — **superioris :** *at its upper edge.* — **in manicas non extendunt :** implying, therefore, an opposite arrangement in the case of the men's tunic.

Chapter 18.

Marriage customs.

1. quamquam : *and yet;* the apparent lack of modesty in costume was not accompanied by moral laxity.

4. non libidine : by anticipation of the following clause, the polygamy is viewed as consummated. Supply in translation, " who resort to polygamy." — **plurimis nuptiis ambiuntur :** *are the objects of sollicitation for plural marriage.* As an historical instance of a polygamous marriage initiated for reasons of state, recall Caesar, *Bellum Gallicum* 1. 53: *duae fuerunt Ariovisti uxores altera Norica, regis Voccionis soror, quam in Gallia duxerat a fratre missam.*

5. dotem non uxor marito : in contrast with the classical Greek and Roman practice, according to which the marriage of a portionless woman was well nigh unthinkable. The action in the *Trinummus* of Plautus centers in such a proposal, regarded by the brother and the guardian of the bride-to-be as spelling family disgrace ; see, *e.g.*, line 612, *flagitium quidem hercle fiet, nisi dos dabitur virgini* (' it will be a sin out and out if a dowry isn't given to the maiden '). — **uxori maritus offert :** Tacitus describes inexactly the marriage by purchase, prevalent in his time in Germany. This usage, which in primitive society succeeded marriage by capture, was in vogue in Homeric Greece and existed among the Thracians in the time of Xenophon, to whom Seuthes says, *Anabasis* 7. 2. 38, ' If you have a daughter, I will buy her according to the Thracian custom.' The *dos* constituted the price paid for the transfer of the woman from the *potestas* of her father to that of her husband ; it was not paid to her, as Tacitus says, but to her parents. The inaccuracy of Tacitus is due to his desire to make the contrast between Roman and German practice as pointed as possible. A later step involved giving the portion or a part of it to the bride.

6. munera: repeated for the sake of emphasis. Such anaphora is a favorite device of the poets, notably at the ending and the beginning of lines; *e.g.* Catullus, 63. 8–9:

> *niveis citata cepit manibus leve typanum,*
> *typanum, tubam Cybelles, et cet.*

(' in his hands white as snow he quickly grasped the light tympanum, the tympanum, trumpet of Cybele '). Vergil, *Aeneid* 2. 405–6:

> *ad caelum tendens ardentia lumina frustra,*
> *lumina, nam teneras arcebant vincula manus.*

7. ad delicias muliebres: a disparaging side glance at the jewels and the other articles of adornment prized by the bride of civilization.

9. in haec munera: *on proviso of these gifts.*

10. armorum aliquid viro adfert: a sword was given, not by the bride but by the bride's father, in token of the power of life and death which the husband was henceforth to possess over her. The interpretation put by Tacitus on the custom is that which best accords with his idealizing tendency.

A spear figured in the Roman marriage ceremony, not, however, as a gift; the hair of the bride was parted with it, a ceremony ordinarily explained as a reminiscence of the days of marriage by capture.

11. haec arcana sacra: Tacitus alludes to the traditional form of patrician marriage, the *confarreatio*, a ceremony which partook of a sacramental character and was celebrated with religious rites (*arcana sacra*) in the presence of the *Flamen Dialis*. — **coniugales deos**: the divinities invoked in the marriage formula, such as Jupiter Farreus, Juno Pronuba, and the agrarian deities Tellus, Picumnus, and Pilumnus; in the time of the Empire we hear also of Venus, Suadela, and Diana as patron goddesses of marriage.

12. extra virtutum' cogitationes: *untouched by the concerns of heroism.* It is interesting to compare with the thought of this context one of the explanations hazarded by Plutarch, *Roman Questions* 87, as to why the hair of the Roman bride was parted with a spear: ' Is it that they may instruct them that they are to dwell with husbands that are soldiers and warriors and that they should put on such ornamental attire as is not luxurious but plain? ' Chauncy's translation.

14. auspiciis: an apposite word, suggested by the place of the *auspicia* in the Roman marriage ceremony. Originally the auspices were taken as an essential preliminary to the rite; in the time of Cicero divination from entrails had superseded the *auspicia* proper and even this was not invariably resorted to; see *De Divinatione* 1. chap. 16. In the Empire, though the practice itself seems to have fallen into disuse, traces of it survived in the participation in the ceremony, as sponsors and witnesses, of the so-called *auspices nuptiarum*. Hence *auspiciis* here should not be translated merely *by the beginning* but rather *by the initial ceremonial. Incipientis* is redundant.

17. denuntiant: *proclaim*.

18. quae: serving in a double capacity as object of *accipiant* and subject of *referantur*.

Chapter 19.

Feminine morality; moral standards.

Throughout the following eulogy of German womanhood, Tacitus by implication is arraigning the decadent morality of Roman society.

1. ergo: marking the features of German life set forth in this chapter as consequent on the sanctity of the marriage relation discussed in the preceding chapter. — **saepta pudicitia agunt**: *they live a life of sheltered modesty.* — **spectaculorum . . . inritationibus**: the public spectacles and luxurious banquets were prolific sources of social depravity under the Empire, as many allusions in the poets and satirists show. See Friedländer, *Roman Life and Manners under the Early Empire*, Eng. Trans., 1, p. 245 f.

3. litterarum secreta: *secret missives;* Tacitus does not say that the Germans did not know how to write, though there is reason to believe that this was the case, generally speaking, but simply that they were not schooled in the use of the *billet doux* as an instrument of intrigue. Ovid's *Amores* 1. 11 and 12 are literary illustrations of the device.

5. praesens et maritis permissa: the *Lex Iulia*, enacted by Augustus in 17 B.C., restricted such private vengeance in Rome and subjected the offender to due process of criminal law. In earlier times the husband, by virtue of the *patria potestas* which he possessed, could slay a guilty wife at once.

6. nudatam . . . expellit: according to Maspero, *Peuples de l'Orient*, 1, p. 736, in ancient Chaldaea an adulterous woman, clothed only in a loin cloth, was driven into the street, and left to the mercy of the passers-by.

7. publicatae . . . venia: *for the surrender of chastity meets with no mercy.* The harshness, as judged by the Roman standards of the time of Tacitus, of the punishment meted out to the adulteress, is explained by this generalizing comment on the uncompromising attitude of the Germans toward the fallen woman, married or single. This attitude is elucidated by the context following.

8. aetate: *youth.*

9. invenerit: the subject for the moment uppermost in the mind of Tacitus is the unmarried woman who has lost her virtue; naturally, he intended that the reader should regard it as self-evident in the light of the context that the denounced *adultera* could not hope for a second husband. — **nemo . . . ridet**: a pessimist's side thrust at the Roman code of social ethics.

10. saeculum: *the spirit of the times* or *the way of the world;* cf. Pliny, *Epistulae* 10. 97 : *nam et pessimi exempli nec nostri saeculi est* (' for (such an act) is of the nature of the worst precedent possible and is not in accord with the spirit of our age '). — **melius quidem adhuc**: *still better even;* supply *faciunt* or a like verb.

With the frequency of divorce and remarriage in Roman society in mind, Tacitus speaks with approval of the lengths to which conjugal loyalty was carried by the women — nothing is said as to the men — of certain states in which the remarriage of widows was frowned on. Such imposition of wifely loyalty has expressed itself variously among different races, in the social neglect and degradation of the widow, in her enforced suicide; cf. the *Suttee* of the Hindoo widow.

12. semel **transigitur**: *an end is made once for all.* The spirit of devotion which kept a woman content with one marriage was highly approved by the Romans themselves in early times (see Valerius Maximus, 2. 1. 3), nor was appreciation of it entirely foreign to social ideals under the Empire, as the frequent recurrence in epitaphs of the epithet *univira* shows; cf. also Propertius in the beautiful *Consolatio Quintiliae* 4. 11. 36; also 67–68:

> *filia*
> *fac teneas unum nos imitata virum*

(' Daughter   look to it that in emulation of me, you cleave to one husband '). Such writers as Juvenal, with his reference, *Satires* 6. 229–230, to a woman who had eight husbands in five years, and Seneca, in his satirical allusion to women reckoning years by their husbands instead of in terms of the consuls, present a too dark picture; cf. Seneca, *De Beneficiis* 3. 16.

14. longior **cupiditas**: *nursing of desire.*

15. tamquam . . . **ament**: they are enamored not with the man *qua* man, but with the idea of marriage which he makes possible; cf. our English saying " to be in love with love." — **numerum liberorum finire**: in contrast with the race suicide rife in Roman society under the Empire. It was to offset this menace that Augustus enacted a body of laws, including the celebrated *Lex Papia Poppaea* (cf. on *Agricola* 6. 3), by which he sought to foster parenthood by imposing disabilities on celibates and childless persons, and conferring prerogatives on fathers of families.

16. adgnatis: here in the sense of younger children, born after the heir. — necare **flagitium habetur**: in his zeal for idealizing German folkways at the expense of Roman, Tacitus has fallen into misstatement. Exposing infants at the behest of the father — a practice the legal justification of which was a blot on ancient civilization in general — obtained among the Germans as well as elsewhere. On the reported prevalence of infanticide in Rome in the days of the Empire, see Lecky, *History of European Morals*, 2. chap. 4. p. 24 f.

18. bonae **leges**: such as the *Lex Papia Poppaea;* for the sentiment compare Propertius, 4. 11. 47–48:

mi natura ded*it leges a sanguine ductas*
ne possem melior iudicis esse metu
(' to me nature gave a code derived from my blood, making me
a woman beyond the possibility of betterment through fear of
a judge ').

Note the epigrammatic and rhetorically balanced structure of
this closing sentence of the chapter.

Chapter 20.

Child nurture; laws of relationship and inheritance.

1. in omni domo: among rich and poor alike. — **nudi ac
sordidi**: to take these epithets literally is not to do violence to
the probabilities. This is the system (?) of child nurture usual
among a primitive people, and that, after all, is what the Germans of Tacitus were. Note in this connection the following:
" Children of the Eskimo on the eastern coast of Greenland go
naked in the house until they are sixteen years old. Then they
put on the *natit* (loin-cloth) and that is the only thing worn in
the house by adults. It is the custom of wearing fur next the
skin (see note on **17. 3**) which compels them to go naked in the
house." W. G. Sumner, F*olkways*, p. 441.

2. quemque mater . . . **alit**: referred to in *Dialogus* 28 as an
old-time Roman virtue. The discontinuance of this practice
was deplored by educational theorists, especially because of the
supposed deleterious effects on the mentality and character of
the rising generation incurred by intrusting children to the care
of hirelings; cf. A*gricola* 4. 8; *Dialogus* 29; Plutarch, *Discourse on the Training of Chil*dren, chap. 5.

3. nec **ancillis ac nutricibus**: cf. the language of *Dialogus* 28:
*Nam pridem suus cuique filius ex casta parente natus, non in
cellula emptae nutricis sed gremio ac sinu matris educabatur*
(' In the good old days, every man's son, born in wedlock, was
brought up not in the chamber of some hireling nurse, but in
his mother's lap and at her knee ' — Peterson); 29: *At nunc
natus infans delegatur Graeculae alicui ancillae* (' Nowadays, on
the other hand, our children are handed over at their birth to
some silly little Greek serving-maid ' — Peterson). — **dominum**:
strictly, in old-time Southern parlance, the " young master."

4. educationis deliciis: *by any refinements in their up-bring-ing.* As a rule, in primitive societies the slave is treated as only a slightly inferior member of the family. See for a full discussion of this topic Westermarck, *The Origin and Development of the Moral Ideas,* vol. 1, p. 678 f. The *verna,* or house-born slave, was proverbially a privileged character in Roman private life; cf. the picture of the idyllic life in Tibullus, 1. 5. 25–26:

> . *consuescet amantis*
> *garrulus in* d*ominae ludere verna sinu,* et seq.

(' the prattling home-born slave child will be wont to frolic on the lap of the doting mistress ').

5. inter eadem pecora: as travelers can testify, among the peasantry of many a country to this day " quarters for man and beast " are not separate. — **humo:** the dirt floor of the homestead.

6. sera   venus: according to Caesar, *Bellum Gallicum* 6. 21, marriage before the twentieth year was strongly discountenanced.

7. nec   festinantur: another contrast with Roman custom; Agricola's daughter was thirteen when Tacitus married her (see note on *Agricola* 9. 24), and instances of earlier marriages are plentiful.

8. eadem iuventa: *i.e.* the age of maturity was reached no sooner by women than by men, a condition of affairs grounded on arbitrary theory and not on physiological facts. In an old poem, entitled *Dietrichs Flucht,* thirty years is mentioned as the marriageable age of both sexes in the good old times; a similar view held good in Italy in the thirteenth century; see Weinhold, *Die Deutsche Frauen in dem Mittelalter,* 3d ed., p. 266. — **pares:** sc. *aetate.*

9. sororum filiis . . . apud avunculum   honor: at different periods of culture and among various races of mankind, descent and inheritance have been reckoned through the maternal side. This system, termed formerly the matriarchate, but recently and more correctly the mother-right or the mother-family, existed, *e.g.* among the Lycians of Herodotus, 1. 173, among the ancient Arabs (see Robertson Smith, *Kinship and*

Marriage in Early Arabia) as well as other Semitic races, and is found in certain savage and semi-civilized peoples at the present time. Under it the mother's brother (*avunculus*) naturally tends to stand in such a close relation to his sister and her children as is described in this sentence. *E.g.* a modern Abyssinian proverb runs " the maternal uncle has children without begetting them " (communicated to the editor by Professor E. Littmann).

The present context has been frequently cited as proof that the mother-right prevailed among prehistoric Germans and survived in the time of Tacitus to the degree here indicated. However, the existence of the institution among Indo-Europeans has not been certainly demonstrated. It is safer, in the present state of our knowledge, to assume that the position occupied by a brother as " next friend " of his sister and her offspring, originated in the desirability of a wife and her children having some representative to champion their interests against a too rigorous exercise of the husband's *potestas*, or, in the event of his death, to maintain a son's right of inheritance against his father's kinsfolk. The fact that after the death of her father a maiden passed legally into the guardianship of her eldest brother, may also have been a contributory cause.

10. ad: not infrequently in Latin of various periods, *ad* has the sense of *apud; e.g.* Plautus, *Captivi* 699, *in libertatest ad patrem in patria;* Livy, 7. 7, *neque segnius ad hostes bellum apparatur;* Tacitus, *Annales* 1. 8, *iactantia gloriaque ad posteros.* Here the change is made for variety's sake. — **quidam**: certain tribes of Germany or the leaders who represent them in negotiations.

12. tamquam . . . teneant: expressing the conviction of the persons represented in *quidam*. Make this fact clear in translation.

13. domum latius: as tending to secure the loyalty of both the paternal and the maternal side of the house.

14. tamen: notwithstanding the intimate relation existing between maternal uncle and nephew, the privileges of inheritance and succession were not affected. These were resident in the paternal line. — **nullum testamentum**: inheritance, which followed the male line, was regulated by consanguinity only, and legacies to others than kinsmen were unknown.

17. adfinium: *connections by marriage.* — **gratiosior**: *the more an object of esteem.*

18. nec ulla orbitatis pretia: in Roman society the childless rich were overwhelmed by the blandishments of would-be heirs. Allusions to the legacy hunter or *captator* are commonplaces in the literature of the Empire; Horace, *Satires* 2. 5, is a jocular *ars captandi* " *testamenta senum* " and the Regulus of Pliny, *Epistulae* 2. 20, is a type of the profession.

Chapter 21.

Blood feuds; hospitality.

Friendships and enmities are also objects of inheritance; herein lies the nexus between this chapter and the preceding.

1. inimicitias: the later Latin equivalent in the German laws was *faida*, whence Mod. Ger. F*ehde*, Eng. *feu*d. The doctrine that the infliction of vengeance is 'the right and the duty of the kinsmen of the victim was axiomatic in early stages of society and has been perpetuated among races who have attained a high degree of culture, *e.g.* the ancient Greeks and the Japanese. The Corsican vendetta, the family feuds of the Scottish clans, and of their descendants, the southern mountaineers in this country, are modern survivals of this custom of blood revenge. This subject is discussed at length by Westermarck, *The Origin and the Development of the Moral Ideas*, chap. 20.

2. necesse est: *it is obligatory.* — **nec**: a negative adversative — *and yet . . . not.*

3. luitur: in the evolution of society it was seen that the acceptance of material compensation in the form of cattle, money, or other property offered a means of escape from the dangers and inconveniences attendant on the view that an injury can be canceled only by the infliction of a like injury. Blood revenge or acceptance of compensation was ordinarily at the option of the injured party. The German term, W*ergel*d, applied to this compensation, Latin *satisfactio, compensatio,* means ' man-price.' The system can only flourish where there is a certain amount of wealth. — **armentorum ac pecorum**:

Wergeld was naturally computed in terms of the prevalent standard of valuation. Compensatory damages varied with the rank of the victim.

4. universa domus : responsibility in a blood feud is collec‑ tive and rests on the family ; hence all those concerned share in the settlement.

5. **utiliter in publicum** : characterizing the compensatory system as a whole, not simply the detail last mentioned, *satis‑ factionem . . . domus.* Compare with this context the following comment of Westermarck, *op. cit.*, p. 485 : "Whilst the carry‑ ing out of the doctrine a ' life for a life ' often leads to pro‑ tracted hostilities between the parties, compensation has a tendency to bring about a durable peace. For this reason it is *to the interest of society at large* (editor's italics) to encourage the latter practice."

6. **iuxta** : *when coupled with;* the absence of state control would tend toward individual excess in enmity.

7. **convictibus et hospitiis** : the former word refers broadly to occasions of good cheer, convivial entertainments ; the latter to the reception of strangers, a topic to which the rest of this chapter is devoted. — **effusius indulget** : unquestioning hospi‑ tality is the rule in primitive societies. The twofold meaning resident in Greek ξένος, Latin *hospes*, ' stranger and guest,' attests the original dominance of the custom. On the other hand Latin *hostis*, akin etymologically to German *Gast*, meant first ' stranger,' then ' enemy.'

Unlike other social virtues, hospitality tends to decline with the advance of civilization, when increased facility of inter‑ course between communities makes strangers less of a novelty, and the establishment of public places of entertainment renders private benevolence less essential.

8. **nefas habetur** : cf. Caesar, *Bellum Gallicum* 6. 23. 9 · *hospitem violare fas non (Germani) putant. Qui quacumque de causa ad eos venerunt, ab iniuria prohibent, sanctos habent hisque omnium domus patent victusque communicatur.*

In the code of hospitality kindly treatment of the guest is a moral obligation, sometimes extended so far as to necessitate the reception and inviolability of a foe. Frequently, the stranger is regarded as under the protection of the gods and hence is sacrosanct; we may recall the Ζεὺs ξείνιοs of the Greeks and the *dii hospitales* of the Romans, also "The Lord preserveth the strangers," *Psalms* 146. 9, and *Odyssey* 9. 270: Ζεὺs . . . ξείνιοs ὅs ξείνοισιν ἅμ' αἰδοίοισιν ὀπηδεῖ ('Zeus . . . protector of guests, who attendeth on revered stranger guests').

9. pro fortuna . . . epulis **excipit:** "Quelque encombrée que soit une hutte et si reduite que soit la quantité d'aliments dont on dispose, le nouvel arrivant est toujours assuré d'avoir une place près du foyer et une part de la nourriture." Hyades and Deniker, *Mission Scientifique du Cap Horn*, VII. 243. — **cum defecere:** folk custom, instead of governing the length of a guest's stay by the contents of the host's larder only, frequently sets a definite limit for the dispensing of hospitality. Three days and nights was a period accepted by several races, including the later Teutons.

13. quantum ad ius hospitis: cf. *quantum ad gloriam, Agricola* 44. 8. — **abeunti:** so often in the Homeric poems it is etiquette for the host to speed the departing guest with gifts, ξεινήια, (*e.g. Odyssey* 4. 589 f.; 24. 273 f.; 285) which, however, are usually not subject to the option of the guest, although in 4. 600 Telemachus excuses himself from accepting the horses and chariot offered by Menelaus, who thereupon substitutes other presents, 4. 612 f.

14. moris: sc. *est.* — **poscendi in vicem:** an exchange of presents between host and guest, not, however, the result of stipulation, is mentioned in *Iliad* 6. 218. Among some peoples superstitious dread of the malevolent power with which it is believed a stranger is endowed, prevents the acceptance of gifts from him, lest they may contain the potency for evil.

15. facilitas: *freedom from constraint.* — imputant: *set down to their credit, i.e.* the donors are not actuated by the spirit of *quid pro quo.*

16. victus . . . comis: many editors regard this sentence as a mere summary of the thought of the whole paragraph and have taken exception to it as superfluous and weak. Rather, it should be joined closely in thought with the preceding sentence, the asyndeton having the force of *nam;* cf. *Germania* 22. 15–16 : *et salva utriusque temporis ratio est: deliberant . . . constituunt;* *Historiae* 3. 84 : *multis increpantibus, nullo inlacrimante: deformitas exitus misericordiam abstulerat* (' midst the jeers of many, (but) with dearth of tears; (for) the ignominy of his end had removed compassion ').

The sense is : hospitality is not governed by a system of debits and credits, expressed in gifts ; for the intercourse between host and guest is gracious, *i.e.* based on kindliness, not on mercenary considerations.

Chapter 22.

Daily life.

1. statim   lavantur : this chapter aims to present, for the edification of the Roman reader, a series of contrasts between the everyday life of Roman and German. Thus, among the Romans the customary hour for the bath was in the middle of the afternoon just before *cena* (see Becker, *Gallus,* Eng. trans., p. 396), and the variation which naturally followed individual preference and habit, does not seem to have placed it much before noon, *e.g.* in the case of Horace, who bathed before *prandium; ast ubi me fessum sol acrior ire lavatum admonuit* (' but when the too intense heat of the sun has warned me to betake my wearied limbs to the bath '), *Satires* 1. 6. 125. The Elder Pliny had finished his bath by the seventh hour on August 24, *i.e.* 12–1 : 09 P.M. ; cf. Pliny, *Epistulae* 6. 16. 4–5. — **in diem** : among the Romans of all classes the social and business day began, as a rule, with the sun and the serious occupations of the man of affairs were finished correspondingly early ; note the words of Pliny, *Epistulae* 2. 17. 2 : *decem et septem milibus passuum ab urbe secessit (Laurentinum), ut peractis quae agenda fuerint salvo et composito die possis ibi manere* (' (my Laurentine villa) is distant seventeen miles from the city ; hence, after dispatching the program of business, one can take up one's sojourn there and not lose the day's work or leave it unfinished ') ; Horace, *Epistulae* 1. 17. 6, mentions sleep *primam in horam* as a comfortable night's rest. The hardships which the necessity for early rising inflicted on the client and the professional man are a favorite topic in the literature of the Empire; cf. Horace, *Satires* 1. 1. 10; 2. 6. 34; Juvenal, *Satires* 5. 19–23.

2. saepius calida: sc. *quam aqua frigida*. The language of Tacitus does not forbid the reader to assume that, at least at certain seasons of the year, the Germans resorted to bathing in the rivers. Hence there is no essential variance with Caesar's account, *Bellum Gallicum* 4. 1. 10: *ut frigidissimis locis . . . (Suebi) lavarentur in fluminibus;* 6. 21. 5: *(Germani) . . . promiscue in fluminibus perluuntur.* The different purpose of each author leads him to emphasize different features of the Germans' practice.

3. separatae . . sedes: contrast the Roman *triclinium*, three guests to each couch.

4. sua cuique mensa: so in the *Odyssey* each banqueter has an individual table; cf. 1. 111; 20. 259, and especially 22. 74, where the suitors use their tables as shields. — **negotia . . . convivia**: as is made clear below, the two were often combined.

5. armati: cf. 13. 1: *nihil autem neque publicae neque privatae rei nisi armati agunt.* — **diem noctemque** continuare: *to make day and night one.* In Rome good form disapproved of the *tempestivum convivium*, a banquet which " began early to last late "; participation in such entertainments was one of the hallmarks of a dissolute life; cf. Cicero, *Pro Archia* 13; Ad *Atticum* 9. 1. 3; Suetonius, *Caligula* 45; Tacitus, *Historiae* 2. 68. The comment of Horace, *Satires* 1. 4. 51 f., on conviviality by daylight, is typical: *At pater ardens saevit quod . . . ebrius (filius) et magnum quod dedecus ambulet ante noctem cum facibus,* et seq. ('But the wrathful father storms because . . . his tipsy son parades the streets with torches before nightfall — a dire disgrace ').

6. crebrae ut inter vinolentos rixae: cf. Horace, *Odes* 3. 21. 1–3 to the wine jar:

> O *nata mecum consule Manlio*
> *seu tu querellas sive geris iocos,*
> *seu rixam et insanos amores*

(' O thou that saw the light with me when Manlius was consul, whether thou hast in store plaints or mirth, whether brawl and frenzied loves '); also *Odes* 1. 18. 8. For this use of *ut* see *Germania* 2. 14.

7. transiguntur: *are dispatched.*

9. adsciscendis principibus: *adopting leaders* or *forming relationships with leaders.* The expression is apparently chosen to emphasize the extent to which power of decision rested with the constituency and is widely comprehensive. Such alliances with *principes* of other tribes, as are mentioned in chap. 14, could come under this head. Probably, however, Tacitus was thinking chiefly of the canvassing at these " business and political dinners " of the merits of the native *principes* available for *duces* in war or for district judges (chap. 12). It is easily conceivable that the party strife existing between rival *principes*, such as is attested by *Annales* 1. 58: *et inieci* (*Segestes*) *catenas Arminio et a factione eius iniectas perpessus sum* (' I both put fetters on Arminius and suffered those placed on me by his partisans '), was a prolific source of " *rixae* " between their adherents on these occasions.

11. simplices: *guileless.* They acted in the spirit of the proverbial *in vino veritas* and would have agreed with the sentiment of Ovid, *Ars Amatoria* 1. 241–242:

> *tunc* (i.e. *post merum*) *aperit mentes aevo rarissima nostra*
> *simplicitas, artes excutiente deo* (*Baccho*)

(' then artlessness, well nigh a stranger to our times, unbars the thoughts, when the god (of wine) doth banish wiles ').

12. ad magnas incalescat: quite in the vein of the famous lines of Burns,

> " Inspiring, bold John Barleycorn !
> What dangers thou canst make us scorn,"

but among the many descriptions, ancient and modern, of "the heart who great and puffed up with this retinue doth any deed of courage and this valour comes of sherris," Bacchylides, Frag. 20 (Blass) has not been improved upon; ' That power sends a man's thoughts soaring; straightway he is stripping cities of their diadems of towers, — he dreams that he shall be monarch of the world; — . . . such are the raptures of the reveller's soul.' Jebb's trans.

13. adhuc : *still;* there is a contrast between the candor of the simple-hearted Germans in their cups and the reticence of the sophisticated and politic man of civilization ; see Ovid, *Ars Amatoria* 1. 241–2, quoted above, *aevo rarissima nostro simplicitas.* — secreta pectoris, **et seq.** : a sentiment as old as Homer, ' wildering wine that sets even a wise man on to sing aloud . . . and uttereth a word that were better left unsaid,' *Odyssey* 14. 463 f., and often repeated since but never more effectively than by Horace ; cf. *Odes* 3. 21. 14 f. :

> *tu sapientium*
> *curas et arcanum iocoso*
> *consilium retegis Lyaeo*

(' thou dost unveil the broodings of the wise and the secret purpose by the spell of the jocund Releaser ') ; see also *Epistulae* 1. 5. 16 : *quid non ebrietas designat? Operta recludit,* et seq. (' what doth not the cups disclose? They reveal the covert thought ') ; cf. also *Satires* 1. 4. 89.

These parallels have been quoted to show how through this whole context Tacitus writes in the language and presents the sentiments of the literature of conviviality ; the parallels furnish the best commentary on the passage.

14. retractatur : *(the discussion) is reopened.*

15. salva . . . ratio est : *the regard belonging to each occasion is preserved.*

16. nesciunt : in poetry *nescire* is often used as a synonym of *non posse*, hence here *nesciunt* commended itself as a variant of the following *non possunt;* cf. Vergil, *Georgics* 3. 83–4 : *tum, si qua sonum procul arma dedere, stare loco nescit (equus)* ; Horace, *Ars Poetica* 390 : *nescit vox missa reverti;* for a similar collocation of the two verbs see Propertius, 1. 5. 23–4 : *nec tibi nobilitas poterit succurrere amanti; nescit Amor priscis cedere imaginibus* (' nor will high lineage have power to rescue thee when thou dost love ; Cupid knoweth not surrender unto ancestral portraits '). — **dum** errare non **possunt** : an overstatement for the sake of an epigrammatic ending. An interesting parallel to this whole context is furnished by Plutarch's discussion, *Symposiaca* 7. 9 and 10, as to the wisdom of following the custom of the Persians and " debating state affairs midst the cups."

Chapter 23.

Food and drink.

1. potui umor ex hordeo: *beer*; cf. the οἶνος κρίθινος of the ancient Armenians, Xenophon, An*abasis* 4. 5. 26, and Vergil's allusion to the national beverage of the northern peoples, *Georgics* 3. 379–380:

> *hic noctem ludo ducunt et pocula laeti*
> *fermento* (yeast or fermented grain) *atque*
> *acidis imitantur vitea sorbis.*

— frumento: i.e. *wheat*, in practice the usual connotation of *frumentum*, since this was the grain ordinarily served out as rations in the Roman armies and given in doles to the citizens.
— **in . . . similitudinem vini**: cf. Vergil's *pocula imitantur vitea.*

2. proximi ripae: this same expression is used in chap. 17. 5–6.
— **vinum mercantur**: Caesar, *Bellum Gallicum* 4. 2. 6, writes of the Suebi of his time: *vinum omnino ad se importari non patiuntur quod ea re ad laborem ferendum remollescere homines atque effeminari arbitrantur.* The German words relating to the culture of the grape and the manufacture of wine are mostly Latin derivatives: *e.g. Wein, vinum; Most, mustum; Keller, cellarium,* et cet.

3. poma: not only the fruits of trees, such as apples, pears, and the like, but also berries and nuts. There is no equally comprehensive word in English. — **recens**: the Romans shared the predilection of the modern palate for meat rendered tender by " hanging " and even tended to carry the appreciation of a gamey flavor to extremes.

4. lac concretum: curds, clotted cream, et cet.; on the menu of the ancient Germans cf. also Caesar, *Bellum Gallicum* 6. 22. 1: *maior pars eorum victus in lacte, caseo, carne consistit.* — **blandimentis**: *whets* and sauces such as figured extensively in the Roman bill of fare; note the list in Horace, *Satires* 2. 8. 8–9:

> *rapula, lactucae, radices, qualia lassum*
> *pervellunt stomachum, siser, allec, faecula Coa*

('rapes, lettuce, radishes, such condiments as stimulate the jaded stomach, skirret, fish-pickle, tartar-lees of Coan wine').

7. haud minus facile . . . vincentur: this sentence was obviously written to bring the chapter to an epigrammatic close,

G

hence the meaning of *facile* should not be pressed. Tacitus did not mean that the Germans could be conquered easily in any case, only that alcohol would be as effective against them as would armed force; the introduction of luxury and dissipation is mentioned also as an agency of conquest in *Agricola* 21. 10 f.

Chapter 24.

National amusements and games.

1. **coetu:** *social gathering.*

2. **ludicrum:** *a sport.*

3. **infestas:** the weapons were poised so as to point at the dancers or leapers. Analogous exhibitions sometimes occurred at Greek and Roman feasts; cf. Xenophon, *Symposium* 2. 11, where a dancing girl performs acrobatic feats in and out from a circle of upright swords.

4. **non in quaestum:** in contrast with the professional entertainers at Rome. *In* has its frequent final force.

5. **quamvis:** its force is limited to *audacis;* cf. the use of *quamquam* in *Agricola* 1. 3. — **lasciviae:** *abandon.* — **pretium est voluptas:** the spear dance, in origin at least, was probably a religious ceremony connected with the cult of the war god.

6. **quod:** the antecedent is the idea contained in the following words. — **inter seria:** *as a serious occupation,* whereas at Rome gambling was a feature of debauchery and the gamester was coupled, in the opinion of the respectable, with offenders of the worst sort; cf. Cicero, *Catiline* 2. 23: *in his gregibus omnes aleatores, omnes adulteri, omnes impuri, impudicique versantur;* Juvenal, *Satires* 11. 176: *alea turpis, turpe et adulterium mediocribus.* In Republican times dicing was forbidden by law and Justinian placed legal restrictions on it in the late Empire; at the most, it was countenanced as a diversion permissible at times of festivity, such as the *Saturnalia,* and excess exposed even an emperor to criticism, as we learn from Suetonius, *Augustus* 71. For a satirist's account as to its prevalence in the society of Rome at the time of Tacitus, see Juvenal, 1. 87–93.

8. **extremo ac novissimo iactu:** *final, decisive throw.*

9. **corpore:** *life.* Power of punishment, even to killing, was vested in the master. Gambling for high stakes is frequently

a racial trait of barbarous peoples; cf. for example, Francis Parkman, *The Jesuits in North America*, Introd. xxxvi: "Like other Indians, the Hurons were desperate gamblers, staking their all, — ornaments, clothing, canoes, pipes, weapons, and wives." — voluntariam: in contrast to bondage incurred under pressure of some external agency, as capture in war or infliction of legal penalty.

10. iuvenior: this form occurs only in writers of the Empire. — adligari: if we may judge from other passages in which this compound occurs, this word was applied in a technical sense to fettering the hands and feet of slaves.

12. per commercia: cf. *Agricola* 28. 15, *per commercia venumdatos (servos)*; 39. 5, *emptis per commercia*.

As a rule in slave-holding races, intra-tribal slaves are treated better than extra-tribal. In particular, slave debtors, the head under which the slaves of the class here described, would naturally fall, are treated with lenience, being often as little restricted in their movements and existence as they would be if they were free agents. Among the Israelites, for example, the native who had lost his liberty through debt met with far more consideration than slaves of foreign extraction; see *Levit.* 25. 39 f.

On the other hand, it is easy to see how the relation of master and slave brought to pass in the way described between two men who had been social equals, would be a painful and difficult situation. The transfer of "*servi huius condicionis*" into a bondage removed from their erstwhile life, and the motives which, according to Tacitus, actuated their sale, find an instructive analogy in old Roman practice. That a Roman should be slave to a fellow-citizen was repugnant to Roman ideas; so it was that in *Tabula* 3 of the *Laws of the Twelve Tables* it was ordained that, after the third day, the debtor who had been made over to his creditor should be punished with death or sold abroad, *i.e. trans Tiberim;* see Mackenzie, *Studies in Roman Law*, p. 94.

Chapter **25.**

Slaves and freedmen.

1. ceteris servis: turning from the special type of slave, whose treatment forms a case apart, to the status of the ordinary slave population. — descriptis: *marked out.*

2. familiam: *the staff of slaves* belonging to an establishment. The complexity of Roman private life naturally called for a specialization of functions as between the *familia urbana* and the *familia rustica* and within these two groups, especially the former; see Sandys, A *Companion to Latin Studies*, Art. 539. — **suam . . . sedem . . . regit**: an analogous arrangement was in vogue in Italy, where, for a consideration in money or produce, a slave might hold and work a parcel of land, but only on sufferance of the master. Tityrus, in the *First Eclogue* of Vergil, is such a slave tenant. However, those to whom Tacitus here, in want of a better word, applies the generic term *servi*, were a grade above the Italian slave farmer. They were actually held in serfdom or villeinage, the condition into which in later times slavery in Europe was transformed. Such serfs were bound to the soil and liable to requisition in labor or produce, but preserved their personal freedom.

4. ut colono: the *coloni*, or free tenant farmers, were the class on which the great landowners of the Empire mainly depended for working their estates; see, *e.g.*, Pliny, *Epistulae* 9. 37. The tenant leased a parcel of land on shares (*colonus partiarius*) — herein lies the point of resemblance with the German serf — or for a money rental (*colonus qui ad pecuniam numeratam conduxit*). — **hactenus** paret: cf. *Agricola* 10. 19, *hactenus iussum*. In order to throw into relief the harshness of Roman slavery, Tacitus has painted the lot of the German slave in too bright colors; he treats the tenant serf as the typical slave and probably understates his disabilities. Furthermore, as modern ethnological parallels show, the conditions of slavery would not have been the same throughout all Germany, but would have varied greatly among separate tribes, according to their economic position and mode of life.

5. cetera domus officia: *the other services, those of the household.* The implication contained in this sentence, to the effect that the Germans did not have household slaves, is at odds with Tacitus's own statement in chap. 20. 4 and with linguistic evidence, from which it appears that various German words for ' slave,' ' servitor,' like Greek οἰκέτης παῖς, Latin *puer*, denote also ' member of the household,' ' boy,' ' girl,' et cet. We may be sure that in primitive Germany slaves formed a part of at least every well-to-do household and that they were treated as a sort of inferior member of the family. — **verberare . . . ac vinculis et opere coercere**: Roman literature, especially comedy, teems with references to these, the regular punishments inflicted on refractory slaves. *Vinculis* and *opere* are coupled together because the slave condemned to labor in quarry, mill, or on the farm, was shackled and made a member of a chain gang (*compediti*); cf. Cato, *De Agri Cultura* 56; Plautus, *Captivi* 944 : *in lapicidinas conpeditum (eum) condidi* (' I have shackled him and consigned him to the quarry ') is typical.

7. **disciplina et severitate**: = *severa disciplina*. — **impetu et ira**: *a sudden access of fury.*

8. **nisi quod impune est**: otherwise the murderer would have been liable for *Wergeld*. It is by no means the universal rule in systems of slavery that the master cannot be held accountable for killing his slave. In various races and strata of society, custom and law have acted to protect the slave from extreme violence. The power of life and death which the Teutonic master possessed was in ancient times the prerogative of the Roman master, but, before the time of Tacitus, legislation by the emperor Claudius had placed certain checks on the master's power; see Suetonius, *Claudius* 25. The Roman reader would be well aware of this fact. — **non multum supra servos**: they usually remained in a state of clientage and labored under various disabilities.

9. **raro aliquod momentum**: this whole account of the German freedmen is colored by the resentment with which Tacitus and the senatorial class viewed the dominating position usurped in the society and the political life of the Empire by the clever and unscrupulous *libertini* under such emperors as Caligula, Claudius, Nero, and Domitian; see note on *Agricola* 40. 6.

10. **gentibus quae regnantur**: the monarchical states are here distinguished from those ruled by *principes*.

11. **super ingenuos . . . ascendunt**: a comment penned with the conditions holding good in Rome in the principate of the absolutist Domitian in mind, but intrinsically credible, nevertheless. The king's freedmen would be bound to fill important positions in his household and hence to wield influence on policy.

12. impares libertini: *the inferior position of the class of freedmen.* *Libertini* is not merely a synonym for *liberti* but is used in its literal sense to refer to the freedmen as a social class in contrast with *ingenui* above.

Chapter 26.
Financial operations; partition of land; agriculture.
1. faenus agitare: *faenus* here means ' capital ' and the sense of the expression is *to engage in dealings with capital.* — **in usuras extendere**: sc. *faenus; to let it increase with a view to (resultant) interest returns.* The operations of high finance had more than once created trouble in the Roman money market and had necessitated legislation restricting the amount of capital which could be put out at interest, the percentage rate, *et cet.* Tacitus knew that his readers would be cognizant of the abuses in question, and so confines himself to generalities.

2. servatur: *guarded against;* the word is here equivalent to *cavetur;* cf. Livy, 39. 14. 10: *triumviris capitalibus mandatum est ut vigilias disponerent per urbem servarentque ne qui nocturni coetus fierent* (' the board of three in charge of prisons and executions was commissioned to dispose watchmen throughout the city and to guard against the occurrence of nocturnal assemblages '). — vetitum esset: *i.e.* by law, as was the case at Rome. It is self-evident that " crooked " financial operations could not have existed among peoples to whom money was a rarity and barter the rule; hence this context is rather superfluous, a fact overlooked by Tacitus owing to his chronic anxiety to disparage by contrast the ways of civilization. — pro numero cultorum: *in proportion to the number of homesteaders,* i.e. *the free heads of households.* The center of the account of Tacitus is the rural village community which, we have seen in chap. 16, was the typical civic unit among the Germans. Each village had as its environs an expanse of territory, comprising woodland, pasture, and plowland, all of which was owned by the community as a corporation. This difficult and much-discussed sentence is best explained as referring to a system of rotation under which separate tracts of plowland were put under cultivation. From the whole tract of arable land, a section adequate to the needs of the community was sequestrated and worked for a certain period, while the residuum was allowed to lie fallow. How frequently a shift in the field of operations occurred and a different area was broken, Tacitus does not say. This might be after a longer or shorter period, according to the fertility of the tract. Whenever a change was made, the new tract chosen for cultivation naturally had to be commensurate with the number of households in the community, a number which, of course, would be subject to variation.

3. **ab universis**: *by them collectively;* the tenure of land was communal but ·the individual held property rights over the homestead, yard, and the household chattels. In certain primitive civilizations to-day, notably in the South Seas, collective ownership is theoretically absolute and extends to all property and chattels. — **in** vices **occupantur**: *are taken up successively,* literally, *with a view to changes.* As has been said, Tacitus says nothing about any fixed interval of rotation. However, it is evident that the successive occupations of tracts of plowland did not involve a change in the location of the village community. Any such annual series of expropriations as that described by Caesar, *Bellum Gallicum* 6. 22. 2 : *magistratus ac principes in annos singulos gentibus cognationibusque hominum quique una coierunt, quantum et quo loco visum est agri attribuunt atque anno post alio transire cogunt,* an arrangement suitable for a predatory race of nomadic instincts as were the Suebi, whom Caesar had mainly in mind, is out of keeping with Tacitus's picture of German life, a feature of which is permanence of abode, comparatively speaking. Furthermore, the following context implies that tenure of a given territory was continuous or for a period of some duration. — quos **mox** . **partiuntur**: each new tract selected for cultivation by the village corporation was subdivided into quotas to be worked by the individual householders. This system presupposes for the time being a differentiation among the individual parcels and hence marks a development over the conditions depicted by Caesar, who says that, at least among the Suebi, there was a total absence of

defined areas and private holdings; *Bellum Gallicum* 4. 1. 7;
6. 22. 2.

4. secundum dignationem: *on the basis of* rank; when the
land was parceled out among individuals, chieftains and nobles
would receive greater acreage or a choicer plot than those below
them in the social scale. This again is at variance with Caesar,
who implies (6. 22. 4) that all shared alike : *cum suas quisque
opes cum potentissimis aequari videat.*

5. camporum spatia: the large extent of territory held by a
community assured the satisfaction of all accredited claimants
of a share. — arva per annos mutant: *arvum* is land actually
put under cultivation as opposed to *ager*, arable land. It is
hardly possible to understand *arva* as referring to the whole
tract of plowland taken up by the community, as does a recent
critic, and to conclude that this sentence develops the thought
of the preceding *agri . . . occupantur, per annos* elucidating
in vices. The idea contained in *per annos* could easily have
been included at the outset and this would have been in the
manner of Tacitus, who is prone to avoid wasting words. Furthermore, the thought of the two clauses directly preceding the
sentence relates exclusively to the assignments turned over to
individuals and it is natural to suppose that this subject is
continued. We may interpret thus : each year the husband-
man worked a different piece in his apportioned plot and permitted the rest to lie fallow ; this practice was made possible
by the size of each individual's share and was naturally resorted
to because of ignorance of what manure, abundant enough among
them (see c. 5. 4 ; 16. 12), could have accomplished for the enrich-
ment of the soil.

6. nec enim . . . labore contendunt: introducing a contrast between the simple and wasteful methods of German husbandry and
the intensive and diversified operations of Italian agriculture and
horticulture. Translate : *for they do not by work compete, i.e.* their
methods do not measure up to their opportunities. The German
words for fruits and vegetables are mostly of foreign origin, a
fact which goes to show that these articles were not indigenous.

8. seges: *grain.* —imperatur :. the crop is, as it were, a tribute requisitioned by the farmer from his subject, the soil.

The figure is a favorite one; cf. Cicero, *De Senectute* 51: *habent enim* (*agricolae*) *rationem cum terra quae numquam recusat imperium* ('for they (*i.e.* the farmers) have dealings with the land, which never refuses their sway'); also the lines prefixed to the *Aeneid: egressus silvis vicina coegi* | *ut quamvis avido parerent arva colono* ('departing from the woodland (*i.e.* sylvan themes), I compelled the neighboring plowlands to submit to the husbandman, however grasping').

9. totidem: as do the Romans.

10. species: *categories.* — hiems **et** ver **et aestas**: the same three seasons are recognized in the Homeric poems as χειμών, ἔαρ, and θέρος respectively. The primitive division of the year, common to all Indo-European peoples, differentiated winter and summer only.

11. autumni . . . nomen: *Herbst*, 'autumn,' is an original word common to the Germanic stocks. However, it means literally 'harvest-time,' which to a Roman would coincide with summer.

Chapter **27.**

Funeral customs.

1. ambitio: *ostentation.* On the other hand, great pomp always marked the funeral ceremony of a Roman of any standing. So early as the fifth century B.C., the *Laws of the Twelve Tables* incorporated regulations intended to curb extravagance and display in funeral rites. Further sumptuary legislation of this character was enacted by Sulla, who then led the way in disregarding it on the occasion of the funeral of his wife Metella; cf. Plutarch, *Sulla* 35, and on the topic as a whole, Friedländer, *Roman Life and Manners*, Eng. trans., vol. 2, p. 210.

The simplicity of German funerals was in direct contrast to the customs of the Gauls in this regard; cf. Caesar, *Bellum Gallicum* 6. 19. 4: *funera sunt pro cultu .   magnifica et sumptuosa.*

2. certis: *especial.* In the deposits of incinerated wood marking the sites of funeral pyres in the cemeteries of ancient Germany, ashes from the oak, beech, fir, and juniper have been discovered. It has been observed that oak was the wood commonly used in Northwest Germany, fir in the East. — crementur: in the earliest prehistoric period, interment was the sole method of disposing of the dead. The practice of cremation of the corpse and subsequent burial of the ashes, occurring sporadically in the later Stone Age and thereafter increasing in frequency, in the later Bronze Age had developed into a universal folk custom, which, once established, was maintained tenaciously by the Germans through centuries. Tacitus recognizes it as the exclusive method in his time; this, however, was not strictly true for all German lands. Both methods were utilized, sometimes existing side by side in the same region. Nevertheless cremation was the dominant practice in the Roman period; exceptions reflect local usage or family preference.

3. nec vestibus nec odoribus: the opposing Roman custom is often attested; cf. Vergil's description of the funeral of Misenus, which corresponds closely to the ceremonial of his own day, Aeneid 6. 221 f.: *purpureasque super vestes, velamina nota coniciunt . . . congesta cremantur turea dona, dapes, fuso crateres olivo.* At the funeral of Caesar the populace threw robes and ornaments on the pyre, Suetonius, *Caesar* 84. The poet Propertius, stipulating for a simple burial, writes, 2. 13. 23, *desit odoriferis ordo mihi lancibus* (' let me lack the line of dishes incense-laden '). — **sua cuique arma**: to bury or burn with the corpse typical articles of use or adornment is a folk custom which has prevailed among races so far removed from each other as the ancient Greeks and the North American Indians, and was indigenous with the prehistoric Germans. In the graves of the Stone Age the presence of an ax- or spear-head attests the antiquity of the practice of consigning the weapons of the dead to the last resting place. Relics of this character are found more abundantly in the graves of later epochs. In the Bronze Age, after the introduction of cremation, the arms of the dead man were not burned with the corpse but laid beside the urn; often miniature models took the place of the actual weapons. At a relatively late period, reckoned as about 400 B.C., it became customary to place the arms on the pyre, a practice perhaps borrowed from the Celts. The damaged remains were buried together with the ashes of the dead; precautions were taken to bend or otherwise to render

useless such parts of the weapons as were not subject to injury
by the flames.

4. quorundam: naturally the chieftains and the well-to-do.
Archaeological research has fully confirmed the statement of
Tacitus and even supplemented it; the remains prove that not
only the horse but other domestic animals also accompanied the
master to the pyre. The presence, in graves of the Roman
period, of the bones of swine, sheep, and goats probably indicates
that popular belief dictated the propriety of supplying the
departed with means of subsistence in the other world.

In Rome the immolation of animals at the pyre was not unknown; in the time of Tacitus and Pliny, the notorious juris-
consult, Regulus, in the extravagance of his grief at the death of
his son, killed at the pyre the boy's ponies, dogs, and pet birds; see
Pliny, *Epistulae* 4. 2. 3. The tone of the letter sufficiently shows
the abnormal character of the procedure of Regulus as judged by
the ordinary standards of the day. — **sepulcrum caespes erigit:**
a bold, rhetorical locution, justified if not inspired by Seneca,
Epistulae Morales 1. 8. 4: *hanc utrum (domum) caespes erexerit
an varius lapis . . nihil interest* (' it matters not whether this
abode is reared in air a mound of sod or a structure of variegated
marble '). Such mounds, heaped over the ashes of the dead,
were technically called *busta* and were common enough in Italy.
The hillock grave, which was typical in earlier periods of civilization, especially the Bronze Age, was by no means the mode in
the Germany of Tacitus but was utilized at the most only in isolated instances. As a rule, the urn was buried in a shallow
cavity and the ground over it was raised only to a slight elevation
above the surrounding level. The *bustum* of sod, familiar to
Tacitus, presented the natural foil to the pyramidal and cylindri-
cal stone sepulchers to be seen in and about Rome, hence is
cited as the tomb *par excellence* of an unpretentious civilization,
by an author who was intent on making a contrast, and not on
presenting details with modern archaeological precision.

5. monumentorum . . . honorem: such as the Pyramid of
Cestius, the Tomb of Caecilia Metella, and other elaborate
mausoleums still to be seen at Rome, especially along the Appian
Way. — **ut gravem defunctis:** Tacitus ascribes to the Germans a

Roman sentiment expressed in the formula *sit tibi terra levis*, a commonplace in epitaphs, and often rendered in paraphrase by the poets, *e.g.* by Propertius, 1. 17. 23–24:

illa meum extremo clamasset pulvere nomen
ut mihi non ullo pondere terra foret

(' she would have called aloud my name over my final dust, (praying) that the earth might rest upon me without weight ').

6. lamenta ac lacrimas cito: it is Tacitus's own ideal as to the conduct befitting mourners with which the Germans are here endowed; cf. *Agricola* 46. 3 f.: *nosque domum tuam ab infirmo desiderio et muliebribus lamentis . . . voces;* see also *Agricola* 29. 2–4.

7. ponunt: = *deponunt.* — **feminis** lugere . . . **viris meminisse**: so, with a slight difference, Charles Kingsley's antithesis: " Men must work and women must weep " (*The Three Fishers*).

9. in commune: *in general.* This context forms the dividing line between the general and the particular in the treatise.

10. accepimus: indicating that his information is gained at second-hand, whether from literary sources or oral tradition; cf. *Agricola* 11. 17. — **instituta ritusque**: the former refers to civic and social usages, the latter primarily to religious ceremonies.ˑ

11. quatenus differant: in so far as individual nations depart from the traits and customs usual to the race. — **quae nationes . . . commigraverint**: this sentence is introductory to chap. 28, the nexus being as follows: Correlative with the topic of German migration into Gaul, the direction of race movement naturally to be predicated because of the superior strength of the Germans at the time at which Tacitus was writing, is, nevertheless, the question as to the opposite possibility, Celtic migration into Germany. To this latter theme Tacitus turns first, as a logical preliminary to the former.

Chapter 28.

Foreign tribes that have entered Germany; German tribes settled on the left bank of the Rhine.

1. validiores: i.e. *quam Germanorum.* — **summus**: *most reliable*, because of his first-hand knowledge of the subject. Caesar's testimony is found in *Bellum Gallicum* 6. 24. 1 : *ac fuit*

antea tempus cum Germanos Galli virtute superarent, . . . propter hominum multitudinem agrique inopiam trans Rhenum colonias mitterent; this passage is also referred to in *Agricola* 11. 14.

2. etiam: said with reference to the countermigration expressed in *quae . commigraverint* above. As a matter of ethnological fact, the so-called Gauls resident in Germany had not migrated thither from Gaul, but were remnants of Celtic peoples who had formerly occupied the territory east of the Rhine and had dominated Central Europe until the pressure of German tribes had largely forced them across the river. — **in Germaniam transgressos**: recall that, in chap. 2, Tacitus has denied the likelihood of migrating tribes being attracted to Germany. He is, however, speaking primarily of migrations by sea in earlier times.

5. promiscuas: *common property.*

6. Hercyniam silvam: in Caesar, *Bellum Gallicum* 6. 25, the vast expanse of wooded mountain ranges extending from the Rhine along the Danube and northeast to the Vistula. Here the mountains separating the German Empire and Bohemia, *i.e.* the Erzgebirge, the Böhmerwald, and the Sudetic Mts., are referred to. — **Rhenumque et Moenum**: together forming a pair and connected with *Hercyniam silvam* by *que. Moenus* is the modern Main.

7. Helvetii: in Caesar's time dwelling in the western part of Switzerland. Formerly they had held Southwestern Germany, including Western and Northern Bavaria, and parts of Franconia, Würtemberg, Baden, and Hesse. Their migrations, which carried them not only to Switzerland but also into Gaul, began in the second century B.C. — **ulteriora**: east of the Böhmerwald.

8. Boihaemi: lit. ' home of the Boii,' whence the modern name of the territory, Bohemia.

9. mutatis cultoribus: the Boii had long since been expelled, and the land which bore their name was, in the time of Tacitus, held by the Marcomanni; cf. chap. 42.

10. Aravisci: they lived west of the modern Budapest, in the territory within the great bend of the Danube. — **ab Osis**: in Northwestern Hungary, north of the bend of the Danube.

11. Germanorum natione: not said with reference to ethnic origin — we learn in chap. 43 that the Osi were Pannonians — but with reference to geographical situation, the lands north of the Danube being included by Tacitus in *Germania;* see chap. 1.

13. incertum est: since the seat of the Pannonian races, of which the Aravisci and the Osi were branches, was south of the Danube, it is more likely that the Osi were the emigrants. In any case the assumption must be based on inference rather than on ethnological data.

14. eadem . bona malaque erant: recall the principle correctly assumed in chap. 2, that trend of migration is affected by the natural advantages possessed by one country over another. Here political conditions are likewise predicated as exerting an influence.

15. Trēvĕri: here begins the treatment of the topic proper, German migration into Gaul. Note that Tacitus here merely quotes the claim of the Treveri and the Nervii to Germanic origin and makes no attempt to support it. In *Historiae* 4. 73 the Treveri are definitely included with the Gauls. As a matter of fact, both peoples were true Celtic nationalities, although they had received accessions of Germanic blood from the assimilation of Teutonic invaders. The Treveri, the most prosperous and flourishing people of the Belgae, lived in the valley of the Moselle. The name of their capital, A*ugusta Treverorum*, survives in the modern Treves or Trier, situated in Rhenish Prussia not far from the border of Luxemburg. — Nervii: Caesar's famous foes ; they dwelt west of the Sambre and were backward in culture as compared with the Treveri. — circa : *in regard to*, a meaning of this preposition frequently found in the writers of the Empire.

16. ultro ambitiosi: *pretentious to a degree.*

18. haud dubie: joined to *Germanorum* attributively.

19. Vangiŏnes, Tribŏci, Nemĕtes: these three tribes occupied the territory on the west bank of the Rhine but not in the order named. The Vangiones were in the vicinity of Worms, the Triboci near Strassburg and the Vosges, while between them, near Speyer, were the Nemetes. All three fought on the side of Ariovistus against Caesar: cf. *Bellum Gallicum* 1. 51. 2. —

Ubii: a powerful tribe, dwelling in Caesar's time in Hesse-Nassau, opposite Coblentz. Having been harried constantly by the Suebi, they put themselves under the protection of Caesar, and it was partly in response to their solicitations that he crossed the Rhine in 55 B.C. Some years later, probably in 38 B.C., although there is some evidence pointing to 19 B.C. as the date of the event, they were transported across the Rhine under the patronage of Agrippa and established in the vicinity of Cologne (*colonia*).

20. **Romana colonia**: in 50 A.D. the capital of the expatriated Ubii, *Oppidum* or *Ara Ubiorum*, was organized as a Roman colony at the instigation of Nero's mother, Agrippina, whose birthplace it was. — **meruerint**: *earned the right.* — **Agrippinenses**: the colony was variously designated *Colonia Agrippinensis* or *-ium*, also, with official formality, *Colonia Claudia Augusta Agrippinensium* and *Colonia Claudia Ara Agrippinensis*.

21. **conditoris**: the word is used in a broad, not in a technical, sense and refers to Agrippina, under whose patronage the colony was organized. According to An*nales* 12. 27, the epithet had a subsidiary significance in perpetuating the memory of Agrippa's relation to the Ubii.

Conditrix is used only in late Latin; even if there had been precedent for the word, Tacitus might well have chosen the form in *-tor* here, as he does in the case of *laudator* in 7. 13–4, *hi* (i.e. *feminae*)   *sanctissimi testes, hi maximi laudatores.*

22. experimento **fidei**: *as a result of their proved loyalty.*

Chapter 29.

Romanized tribes on the right bank of the Rhine; the *Agri Decumates.* .

1. virtute **praecipui**: cohorts of the Batāvi had rendered yeoman service to Rome in the German wars waged by Drusus, Tiberius, and Germanicus; they had also served with great distinction in Britain; cf. *Historiae* 4. 12 and note on *Agricola* 36. 5. In the great revolt under Civilis, 69–70 A.D., they offered stubborn resistance, and, peace having been made on terms favorable to them, they retained immunity from taxation and a privileged position as regards military service.

2. insulam Rheni: before the time of Caesar, the Batāvi had established themselves on the island formed by the Old Rhine, the Waal, and the Maas. — **Chattorum quondam populus**: the origin of the Batāvi and their expulsion from their native haunts are referred to in similar terms in *Historiae* 4. 12. On the Chatti see *Germania* 30. 1.

5. insigne: *token.*

6. tributis contemnuntur: *they do not suffer the slight of taxation.*

7. conlationibus: theoretically, *voluntary contributions*, but sometimes extorted under duress, as, *e.g.*, by Nero after the Fire; *conlationibusque non receptis modo verum efflagitatis provincias privatorumque census prope exhausit* (' as a result of the contributions which he not only received but even demanded, he nearly ruined the provinces and drained the fortunes of individuals ') Suetonius, *Nero* 38. — **in usum proeliorum sepositi**: for a similar use of *seponere* as applied to choice troops, cf. *Agricola* 31. 23: *ostendamus quos sibi Caledonia viros seposuerit.* The Batāvi were expert cavalrymen and swimmers, and were in demand as members of the imperial body-guard.

9. Mattiācorum gens: they lived across the Rhine from Mainz, in the vicinity of the modern Wiesbaden. Their name perhaps survives in Metze, southwest of Kassel. — **protulit enim magnitudo populi Romani**: most critics see in this sentence an allusion to the extension and the fortification of the Roman frontier in Germany carried out by Domitian (see note on *limite acto* below), whose name Tacitus, true to his detestation of that emperor, has suppressed.

However, the locution is quite in the usual manner of Tacitus; cf. *Agricola* 23. 2 : *si   Romani nominis gloria pateretur, inventus in ipsa Britannia terminus.* Secondly, the country of the Mattiāci, famed for its silver deposits and its medicinal springs, had been brought into the sphere of Roman domination by Drusus and Germanicus and had remained under the control of the Empire except during the revolt of Civilis. It may well be that it is to the original occupation of the country of the Mattiāci in the Early Empire that Tacitus here refers.

10. veteres terminos: the Rhine.

12. agunt: the verb has a different shade of meaning with each ablative pair; they live on the German *side* of the Rhine but they *side* with us.

13. adhuc: *still, to this day.* The Batāvi had been expelled from their original abode; the Mattiāci still occupy their native land and have preserved their national consciousness. Hence they are endowed with a more ardent spirit.

16. decumates agros: *tithe lands, i.e.* land leased by the emperor to settlers in consideration of the payment of a tenth of the annual produce. *Decumates,* which occurs only here, is a by-form of the normal term *decumanus.* Its presence, perhaps, is due simply to our author's preference for unusual technical expressions; or it may be that *decumates,* 'tenners,' was the term applied to the inhabitants, the form sanctioned in the local Gallic Latin usage, and then accepted as the official designation of the territory. *Decumas,* like *Arpinas* and similar formations, would be usable either as noun or adjective.

The territory lay between the Rhine, the Main, and the Upper Danube, thus comprising Western Würtemberg and most of Baden. Formerly it had been held by the Helvetians.

18. dubiae possessionis: tenure was insecure because, so long as the frontier was unfortified, the settlers were exposed to the forays of their German neighbors.

19. limite acto: to Tacitus and his readers *limes* in this passage meant the fortified boundary line separating Roman from German territory. Vespasian (69–79) took steps to secure Roman possession of the *Agri Decumates* by extending a military road east from Strassburg and planting *castella* in the valley of the Neckar. The real credit for achieving permanent extension of the Roman frontier north and east of the Middle Rhine belongs to Domitian. As a result of his campaign against the Chatti, 83 A.D., this emperor began a great system of fortifications, which, strengthened and extended by Trajan, Hadrian, and Antoninus Pius, ultimately stretched from Hönningen, situated on the Rhine not far above Bonn, to Hienheim on the Danube, near Regensburg. The original line, after diverging from the Rhine, follows the course of this river and that of the Main to a point north of Frankfort, whence it juts out in a salient converging

H

toward Giessen. Thence it returns in a southerly direction to the Main and is carried south from Worth on the Main, along the Neckar to Rottweil, southwest of Stuttgart. In the principate of Hadrian the *limes* was advanced about 13 miles east of the former line and extended from the Main to Lorch, east of Stuttgart, thence it was continued by the Raetian *limes* to the Danube.

Excavations carried out in Germany and Austria in the last twenty-five years have revealed extensive remains, representing the several periods of fortification. As begun by Domitian, the *limes* consisted of a series of wooden blockhouses and earthen redoubts, in some regions connected by a wattled fence, which must have been designed to serve as an entanglement rather than as a permanently effective barrier. Within the outer line were located at intervals other *castella* as secondary defenses. Hadrian strengthened the works of his predecessors by erecting a strong palisade and by replacing the earlier wood and earth strongholds by forts and watch-towers of stone. The completed line from the Rhine to the Danube was 550 kilometers and more (340+ ms.) in length. — sinus **imperii**: *corner.* As in chap. 1 a projection of land into the water is called *sinus*, so here the term is applied to the angle of Roman territory jutting into the German.

20. provinciae: *Germania Superior;* the formal organization of the lands held by Rome along the Rhine into the separate provinces of Upper and Lower Germany was seemingly the work of Domitian.

Chapter 30.

The Chatti. With this people begins the account of the tribes of Germany proper.

1. ultra hos: the Mattiāci as well as the inhabitants of the A*gri Decumates.* — Chatti: at this time they occupied the land beyond the *limes* between the Lahn and the Werra. Their name survives in modern Hesse. It is evident from the tone of the chapter that Tacitus entertained an admiration for the prowess of the race, which, from the time of Drusus, had come into collision with Roman arms on various occasions. Domitian's campaigns against them were still recent history and the praise bestowed on them by Tacitus is of a piece with his disparagement of Domitian's achievements against them; cf. note on *Agricola* 39. 4. — **Hercynio** saltu : applied, as is the case with *Hercyniam silvam* in chap. 28, to a part of the whole tract. The wooded ranges are a feature of the topography of Hesse.

2. effusis . . . locis : *wide reaches.* The ablative is best explained as local, joined with the idea of situation expressed in the preceding sentence.

3. durant siquidem : giving the reason of the mountainous character of the whole country; *inasmuch as the highlands continue.*

4. rarescunt: *diminish.* — suos : the Chatti are, as it were, the children or protégés of the forest. The overstrained rhetoric of the passage is perilously near " fine writing," as measured by modern standards.

. **5. deponit** : *sets (them) down;* where the hills sink to the plain, the country of the Chatti ends.

6. stricti : *thick-set;* in contrast with the huge frames typical of the Germans as a whole.

˙ **8.** nosse ordines : *they observe rank and formation;* they do not trust to individual prowess but, as we might say, to " teamwork."

9. differre impetus : unlike the proverbial impetuosity of savage peoples, who, as the Roman tactician had learned to his advantage, could generally be tempted to attack irrespective of inferiority of position or difficulty of retreat. — disponere diem : they regulated performance of military duties and details by a fixed order for the day. — vallare **noctem** : *they make the night secure by intrenching themselves;* experience may have taught the Chatti to take this leaf from the Romans' book. It was thus that the Nervii learned to follow Roman methods of fortification; cf. Caesar, *Bellum Gallicum* 5. 42. 2.

11. ratione . . . **concessum** : *vouchsafed* under a studied plan of discipline.

12. robur in pedite : cf. *Agricola* 12. 1 : *in pedite robur.*

13. ferramentis : *intrenching tools.* The arrangement here described was modeled on the Roman system under which the heavy *sarcina* of the legionary comprised rations, *valli*, and other appurtenances of intrenchment.

15. fortuita: *haphazard* — in contrast with *intellegere occasiones* above.

16. parare: *to gain, to obtain;* cf. Cicero, *De Amicitia* 15. 55: *quid autem stultius . . . quam cetera parare quae parantur pecunia, equos, famulos, vestem egregiam, vasa pretiosa: amicos non parare,* et cet. ('moreover, what is denser than to get those other things, such as are purchasable, viz. horses, servants, fine clothing, costly dishes — and not to get friends ').

17. iuxta: like our metaphorical "next door to." — **cunctatio:** in the good sense resident in the epithet *Cunctator* applied to Fabius.

Chapter 31.

A folk usage of the Chatti.

1. et: *etiam.* The thought is: *usurpatum etiam aliis Germ. populis sed raro.* — **usurpatum:** *a practice resorted to;* the participle is in apposition with the following infinitive clause. For a similar usage see *Agricola* 1. 1: *facta moresque posteris tradere, antiquitus usitatum.* — privata **cuiusque audentia:** *as a matter of individual daring.*

2. in consensum vertit: *has developed into a general usage.* — ut primum adoleverint: contrast the practice of the Athenian youths, who wore their hair unshorn until they reached the age of *ephebia*, when their locks were cut for the first time and dedicated to a divinity.

4. nisi hoste caeso: instances in which a vow is made not to cut hair or beard until a certain purpose is brought to pass, are frequent in history and legend. Thus, Civilis vowed not to cut hair or beard until he had won a success against the Romans; cf. *Historiae* 4. 61. The act of Caesar in letting his hair and beard grow until he had taken vengeance on Ambiorix for the destruction of Titurius and his cohorts (Suetonius, *Caesar* 67), is also regularly quoted as another illustration. However, in Caesar's case his unshorn locks may easily be regarded as marking his mourning in the conventional Roman fashion. Suetonius says nothing about a formal vow in this connection, and, if we may judge from Tacitus's characterization of the act of Civilis as *barbarum votum*, such a pledge on the part of Caesar would have been un-Roman.

5. super sanguinem **et spolia**: the vivid description is heightened by the alliteration. For a similar combination of the words in a rhetorical passage see the speech of Civilis *Historiae* 4. 14: *quos ubi spoliis et sanguine expleverint.*

7. ignavis et imbellibus: combined also in chap. 12. 3–4 and in *Agricola* 15. 11.

8. squalor: this word and its cognates, *squalidus, squaleo*, are frequently used of the unkempt, matted condition resulting from neglect of the hair or beard.

There is no real inconsistency involved between this sentence and the account following, from which it appears that the bravest warriors left their hair and beard uncut. Tacitus does not say that only the *ignavi et imbelles* remained unshorn. The members of the warrior brotherhood, whose flowing locks were a token of valor, would be easily distinguishable as a class apart. — **ferreum . . . anulum**: under other circumstances, symbolical of servitude or personal liability, hence a badge of infamy; in this case the ring is plausibly to be regarded as betokening a self-imposed bondage to the war god, Wodan.

10. plurimis: *a goodly number.* — hic . . . habitus: the flowing hair and beard, also the ring.

11. iam . . . canent insignes: *they become already gray with age while bearing these distinctions.*

13. nova: *uncanny.* — nam: explanatory not only of *nova* but also of *prima . . . acies.* Their forbidding exterior, unaltered even in times of peace, is an effective means of striking terror to the hearts of the foe at the first outbreak of hostilities. Hence they are utilized in the front rank. The hideous masks once worn by the Japanese Samurai and the war paint of the Indian may be cited as analogous devices.

Chapter 32.

The Usipi and the Tenctĕri.

1. certum iam alveo: for the moment Tacitus, reversing natural order, is proceeding in thought from the mouth of the

Rhine upstream, and has in mind the single channel of the Middle Rhine as contrasted with the branches into which the river divides in its lower reaches about the *Insula Batavorum.* Most critics understand the contrast to refer to the shifting course of the Upper Rhine after it issues from Lake Constance.

2. Usĭpi ac Tenctĕri : these peoples, two branches of the same stock, are associated in history from the time of Caesar, who in 55 B.C. defeated their attempt to settle west of the Rhine; *Bellum Gallicum* 4. 1–15. After various wanderings they were allowed to establish themselves on the right bank of the Rhine, in the territory opposite Cologne and extending south from the Lippe. See also note on *Agricola* 28. 1.

Tacitus refers through the rest of the chapter to the Tenctĕri only, but merely for brevity. What is said of them applies equally to their kindred, the Usĭpi.

3. super solitum . . . decus : they surpass the measure of prowess, common to all the Germans, in the one detail. — **equestris disciplinae arte** : in this differing from the Chatti, their neighbors. Eight hundred horsemen of the Tenctĕri routed five thousand of Caesar's cavalry. Their tactics consisted in dismounting and stabbing the horses of their opponents from beneath ; cf. *Bellum Gallicum* 4. 12. 2.

6. lusus infantium : so Caesar writes, *Bellum Gallicum* 6. 21. 3 *ab parvulis labori ac duritiae student;* cf. Seneca, *Epistulae Morales* 36. 7 : *si in Parthia natus esset, arcum infans statim tenderet, si in Germania, protinus puer tenerum hastile vibraret* ('if he had been born in Parthia, straightway in his infancy he would bend the bow, if in Germany, forthwith in boyhood he would launch the flexible sapling ').

7. inter : *together with.* — **familiam** : the slaves. — **penates** : the " home," including house and household chattels. — **iura successionum** : *inherited titles to possession, e.g.* the right to a holding of land.

9. maximus natu : it cannot be shown that the right of primogeniture existed as a principle universally observed in the German laws of inheritance. Hence, if the statement of Tacitus as to the procedure among the Tenctĕri be correct, it is an isolated instance. — **melior** : not in a moral but in the physical sense, as we use the expression " better man " with reference to the superiority of one of two combatants over his rival.

Chapter 33.

The Bructĕri, the Chamāvi, and the Angrivarii.

1. iuxta : said from the point of view of one who is going north into the interior, away from the Rhine. — **Bructĕri :** divided by other ancient sources into the Greater Bructĕri and the Lesser ; the latter, whose defeat by the Chamāvi and the Angrivarii is here alluded to, had detached themselves from the rest of their tribe and taken possession of the territory between the Upper Lippe and the Upper Ems. The race was well known to the Romans as a redoubtable foe. At the battle of the Teutoburg Forest they captured the eagle of the 19th Legion but the standard was recovered by a punitive expedition sent among them by Germanicus. The Lesser Bructĕri and their. prophetess, Veleda (see note on 8. 9), had taken a prominent part in the revolt of Civilis. — **occurrebant :** in a geographical sense, equivalent to *habitabant.* — nunc : the event was, therefore, a recent occurrence. This defeat — it by no means amounted to annihilation of the Lesser Bructĕri, as Tacitus reports — occurred in the interval between the year 70 A.D. and the date of this treatise.

2. Chamāvos : their seat was in Holland, southeast of the Zuyder Zee. Their conquest of the Bructĕri enabled them to extend their domain south toward the Lippe ; however, they did not desert their original abode, as is evident from the fact that their name survived in the district called Hamaland in the Middle Ages. — **Angrivarios :** they lived along the Weser in modern Hanover. They retained their tribal unity and their name, shortened to Angrarii, Angarii, down to the time of Charlemagne.

3. penitus excisis : nevertheless they are mentioned in subsequent centuries and continued to hold territory between the Lippe and the Ruhr ; their name survived in the medieval canton Borahtra in Westphalia.

5. ne spectaculo quidem : Tacitus uses both the dative and the ablative after *invidere;* the ablative of the thing is the more frequent construction in the Latin of the Empire.

104 NOTES

7. oblectationi oculisque : best handled in translation as a hendiadys; with *oculis, nostris* or *Romanis* is understood.

Tacitus writes as though the battle were a huge gladiatorial contest, staged by the gods for the benefit of the Roman troops who witnessed it. There was, however, the additional satisfaction that the strife of the Germans helped secure the position of Rome.

9. odium sui : for a similar sentiment as to the value to Rome of dissension among native races, see *Agricola* 12. 4–5 : *nec aliud adversus validissimas gentis pro nobis utilius quam quod in commune non consulunt.* — **urgentibus imperii fatis :** to interpret these words, as has been done by some editors, as implying that the last hour of Rome is drawing near and that the destruction of the Empire by the Teutonic peoples is threatening, is out of keeping with the lively hopes as to the principate of Trajan expressed in *Agricola* 3. 1–4 : *quamquam primo statim beatissimi saeculi ortu . . . augeat . . . cotidie felicitatem temporum Nerva Traianus.* Compare also the statement as to Rome's expansion in *Germania* 29. 9 : *protulit . . . magnitudo populi Romani ultra Rhenum,* et cet. *Fatis* is not *doom*, but *destiny*, "star of Empire," which, of course, carries with it heavy responsibilities. The thought may be rendered : *under the stress of (our) imperial destiny.*

Chapter 34.

The Dulgubnii, the Chasuarii, and the Frisians.

1. a tergo : as the words *a fronte Frisii* indicate, the Chamavi and the Angrivarii are thought of as facing west and northwest toward the sea. Hence *a tergo* means to the south and east. — **Dulgubnii :** east of the Weser, in modern Hanover. — **Chasuarii :** located on the right bank of the Ems, along the Hase.

3. Frisii : they extended along the coast of Holland between the Rhine and the Ems. Their name and their place of abode have remained unaffected by the vicissitudes of history. — **excipiunt :** this verb develops the meaning of ' coming next to.' precisely as does Greek ἐκδέχομαι; see, *e.g.*, Herodotus 4. 39 : ἀπὸ ταύτης (τῆς Περσικῆς ἀκτῆς) ἐκδεκομένη ἡ Ἀσσυρίη καὶ ἀπὸ Ἀσσυρίης ἡ Ἀραβίη (' and next to Persia Assyria, and to Assyria Arabia '). — **maioribus minoribusque :** Tacitus is the only ancient author to mention such an ethnic partition of the Frisians, although the Bructeri were so divided (cf. note on 33. 1), and Pliny the Elder distinguishes the Chauci, closely akin in origin to the Frisians, and their near neighbors on the coast of the North Sea, by the same terminology (*Naturalis Historia* 16. (1). 2). It is probable, that, as has been assumed in the case of the Bructeri, the epithets indicate the separation between a mother stock (*maiores*) and an emigrated colony (*minores*).

4. utraeque: *uterque* is not infrequently used in its plural forms when either of the two members involved denotes a collectivity, or when the members of the pair are closely allied.

5. praetexuntur: the river is conceived as a fringe or edging, comparable to the stripe which bordered the *toga praetexta*.

6. insuper: in addition to the river. — lacns: in ancient times the land of the Frisians was a country of lagoons and salt marshes which nowadays the dikes have reclaimed. The most considerable of the lakes was the Flevo, since the great inundation in the thirteenth century merged in the Zuyder Zee. — **Romanis navigatos**: in the expeditions of Drusus, 12 B.C., Tiberius, 5 A.D., and Germanicus, 15 and 16 A.D.

7. illa: sc. *parte.* — **superesse adhuc**: *are still to be reached;* the explorations had stopped short of the farthest goal possible. Thus Pliny the Elder, *Naturalis Historia* 2. (67). 167, is careful to say : *Septentrionalis vero Oceanus maiore ex parte navigatus est auspiciis* divi *Augusti* ('but the greater part of the Northern Ocean was traversed under the auspices of the deified Augustus')·

8. Herculis columnas: the fame of the Pillars of Hercules at Gibraltar, marking the limits of the known world to the west, and of such rocky barriers as the Symplegades in the east at the entrance of the Black Sea, stimulated the location of analogous portals elsewhere, and naturally in the mysterious north. Some traveler's "yarn" of great cliffs or rocky islets (cf. Pliny, *Naturalis Historia* 6., 199, *ita* (i.e. *columnae*) *appellantur parvae insulae*) doubtless furnished a basis for the tradition.

9. magnificum: *imposing.*

11. Druso Germanico: the brother of Tiberius, the elder Drusus, on whom the epithet Germanicus, to be borne also by his descendants, was conferred after his death. In the words of

Suetonius, *Claudius* 1, *is Drusus . . . dux . . . Germanici belli Oceanum septentrionalem primus Romanorum ducum navigavit* (' this Drusus, while in charge of the war with Germany, first of Roman generals sailed the Northern Ocean '). This feat, as the first venture into unknown waters, put a spell on the popular imagination and is hence singled out here as if it were the only achievement of the kind, at the cost of suppressing mention of later expeditions.

12. nemo temptavit: nevertheless the fleet of Tiberius had operated extensively in these waters in its voyage to the Elbe; cf. note on 1. 4. In 16 A.D. the fleet of Germanicus, son of Drusus, had been wrecked off the Ems and scattered over the Northern Ocean. Failure to mention acquaintance with the North Sea gained under duress, and not as the result of deliberate exploration, is, however, not so surprising as the omission of allusion to the voyage of Tiberius.

Chapter 35.

The Chanci.

1. novimus: *we have been acquainting ourselves with.*

2. redit: *bears back.* According to the geographical notions of the times, the·northwest coast of Germany was conceived of as bending inward in a great curve, ending in the peninsula of the Cimbri (Jutland), which was erroneously located far to the east. — **Chaucorum gens**: they occupied the coast and the adjacent regions of the interior lying between the Ems and the Elbe. They were divided by the Weser into *Maiores* and *Minores.*

3. quamquam incipiat: the subjunctive is the predominant mood with *quamquam* in Tacitus and writers of his period.

4. obtenditur: *abuts on.*

5. in Chattos usque: this junction of the boundaries of the Chauci and the Chatti could have been effected if these two peoples had between them absorbed or expelled the Cherusci, whose power had been on the wane for two generations at this time. As a matter of fact, the Cherusci had been pushed east of the Weser. On the other hand, this account of the extension of the domain of the Chanci to the south is at variance with all other data as to the location of the tribe at this period. The following eulogistic description, in which the characteristics of a humanized and pacifically inclined people are attributed to them, has a suspiciously rhetorical tone. It is possible that, lacking exact information as to the situation and traits of this remote tribe of northwest Germany, Tacitus has done here what he accuses his predecessors of doing in their accounts of Britain, viz. resorting to rhetoric as a substitute for facts.

7. populus . . . nobilissimus: Tacitus's eulogy of the Chanci is notably at odds with the account of them given by Pliny, *Naturalis Historia* 16. (1). 2, who writes as an eye-witness and describes them as a poor fisherfolk, ekeing out a wretched existence in huts, which were situated on dunes and artificial embankments and which were entirely surrounded at high tide. Pliny's narrative doubtless applied only to the fringe of the tribe along the coast and is as much too restricted as the account of Tacitus is too general.

8. iustitia: selected as the chief *motif* in this encomium of the Chauci and developed in the following sentence.

9. impotentia: " the *weakness* of uncontrolled passion," as it has been happily defined. — **secreti**: this epithet would fit the Chanci of the coast, but not those who, according to Tacitus, peopled the *inmensum terrarum spatium* in the interior, and were surrounded by neighbors.

10. nullis raptibus . . . populantur: nevertheless, under the leadership of Gannascus, a chieftain of the Canninefates, the Chanci, after the manner of the Vikings of a later age, had committed a piratical foray against the coast of Gaul in 47 A.D.; cf. *Annales* 11. 18.

11. quod: *the fact that.* — **ut superiores agant**: the verb has here its intransitive sense of *live, exist,* and the clause may be rendered by an abstract noun, *e.g. (their) ascendancy.*

12. non per iniurias: a repetition of the theme *iustitia.*

13. exercitus: this word, when applied to a force of barbarians, connotes an organized army and not an undisciplined host. So in *Agricola* 32. 24 the words of Calgacus, *hic dux, hic exercitus,* voice a claim in keeping with the hortatory spirit of the address. The Chauci, like the Chatti, had adopted Roman methods.

14. et: = *etiam.*

Chapter **36.**

The Cherusci.

1. in latere : *i.e.* on the east. — Cherusci : when at the height of its power, in the first two decades of the first century A.D., the nation of the Cherusci occupied the territory north of the Hartz Mts. between the Elbe and the Weser, and reached to the west beyond the latter river. At the time of Tacitus the Chatti had pushed them east of the Weser.

With their chieftain, the famous Arminius, they were the leading spirits in the war which ended with the destruction of Varus and his three legions in 9 A.D.; it was their effective resistance in the first years of the principate of Tiberius that rendered abortive the ambition of the Romans to extend their limits of domination beyond the Rhine. — **nimiam . . . pacem :** the decline of the power of the Cherusci was due to civil feuds and to the aggression of the Chatti. Nevertheless, it was consoling to the pride of the Romans to contemplate the decadence of the redoubtable foe which had dealt them a blow which had never been adequately revenged. Tacitus's picture of the Cherusci is colored by this consideration.

2. diu . . . inlacessiti : the Cherusci had been in conflict with the Chatti, their inveterate enemies, as recently as 84 A.D., only fourteen years before the *Germania* was written.

4. falso quiescas : *one makes a mistake to remain inactive.* — **manu :** *by force;* cf. the metaphor " the mailed fist."

5. nomina : strictly speaking, not the abstracts themselves but the qualitative epithets implied by them. — **olim :** in the days of their supremacy.

8. Fosi contermina gens : this people is not mentioned elsewhere but was evidently one of the peoples acting under the hegemony of the Cherusci ; cf. A*nnales* 1. 60 : *conciti per haec non modo Cherusci sed conterminae gentes.*

Chapter **37.**

The Cimbri ; résumé of Romano-German relations.

1. eundem . . . sinum : the elbow of land referred to in *ingenti flexu redit,* 35. 2. — **proximi Oceano :** an expression so vague that it is difficult to say whether Tacitus located the remnants of the Cimbri just north of the mouth of the Elbe, in modern Schleswig-Holstein, or in Northern Jutland, where other ancient writers definitely placed them and where, to this day, the names of the districts, Himmerland (Cimbri) and Thythaesyssel (Teutoni), perhaps furnish philological evidence of the presence in olden times of the two peoples. At all events the Cimbri gave their name to the peninsula of Jutland, called by ancient writers *Cimbrorum chersonesus* or *promunturium*.

2. **parva** nunc **civitas**: descendants of a section of the Cimbri which did not join in the great migration. Cimbri are also mentioned as denizens of the " farthest east " in these regions in the time of Augustus, and, together with neighboring tribes, as suing for the friendship of Rome; cf. *Res gestae divi Augusti* (a great inscription found at Ancyra) 5. 14–15. — **gloria**: probably an ablative of specification, balancing a *spatio* implied with *parva*. It may, however, be explained as a nominative.

3. **utraque ripa**: *ripa*, without further definition, refers in Tacitus generally to the Rhine, but also to the Danube according to the context; cf. *Agricola* 41. 6 f.: *tot exercitus in Moesia Daciaque et Germania et Pannonia . . . amissi . . . nec iam de limite imperii et ripa (Danuvii) . . . dubitatum.* Although the Cimbri had wandered along the Danube during several years prior to 113 B.C., the date of their first contact with Roman forces, during the period in which they chiefly menaced Rome their movements were in the west. Hence it is probably the Rhine, ordinarily regarded as the boundary *par excellence* between Roman and German lands, of which Tacitus was thinking; cf. *Agricola* 15. 14–15: *sic Germanias excussisse iugum, et flumine, non Oceano defendi;* Velleius Paterculus, 2. 8: *tum Cimbri et Teutoni transcendere Rhenum.* — **castra ac spatia**: *encampment areas*. The identification of these abandoned fortified sites with camps constructed by the Cimbri rested probably on tradition rather than on exact information. Whether such a migratory horde would take pains to protect itself by bivouacs so durable as to be visible two centuries later, is questionable. Certainly they would not intrench themselves each night, after the thoroughgoing custom of the Romans. In the case of the Chatti in the time of Tacitus, *vallare noctem* is emphasized as a practice exceptional among the Germans; çf. 30. 9.

4. ambitu . . . metiaris: similarly the abandoned camp sites of Varus and his legions, which were discovered by the army of Germanicus in 15 A.D., gave mute testimony as to the size of the forces which built and occupied them; cf. Ann*ales* 1. 61: *prima Vari castra lato ambitu et dimensis principiis trium legionum manus ostentabant* (' the first encampment of Varus by its broad circuit and its regularly marked officers' quarters, gave evidence of the work of three legions '). — **molem manusque**: not necessarily a hendiadys, as often explained. *Moles* is the whole mass of the tribe, including women and children, which the camp would have to be large enough to contain; *manus* refers to the fighting strength.

5. tam magni exitus fidem: *the authenticity of so great an emigration.* The Cimbri and the Teutons are said by Plutarch, *Marius* 11, to have numbered 300,000 fighting men besides the women and the children! An accurate determination of their number is impossible; it doubtless increased in the course of their wanderings. — **sescentesimum et quadragesimum** annum : according to our generally accepted method of reckoning, the Varronian era, Metellus and Carbo were consuls in 113 B.C., on April 21 of which year, A. U. C. 641 began. Sometime during the campaigning season of the year, Carbo by negotiations succeeded in preventing the Cimbri from crossing the Carnian Alps but was subsequently defeated by them. The news of the approach of the Germans may conceivably have reached Rome before April 21, *i.e.* in the closing weeks of the year 640, although such an hypothesis assumes a meticulous regard for chronological minutiae in general foreign to Tacitus and the other ancient historians. The divergence in calculation is at most a matter of months and we may be sure that Tacitus in any case would have preferred the round number; cf. A*gricola* 34. 14, where with greater license forty-two years are expanded into half a hundred.

8. ad alterum . . . Traiani consulatum: 98 A.D., the year in which the *Germania* was written.

10. vincitur: the tense implies that the conquest is not yet complete. If this is a thrust at Domitian and his celebration of a triumph over Germany, as is generally assumed, it is none the less a reminder to Trajan.

11. medio ·spatio: *throughout the interval;* for a like combination of *aevum* and *spatium* see *Agricola* 3. 11 : *per quindecim annos, grande mortalis aevi spatium.*

12. non Samnis . . . ne Parthi quidem: only those enemies that menaced Rome through a considerable period are included — hence, doubtless, the omission of mention of the invasion of Pyrrhus. Note the shifts from singular to plural, from name of people to that of country.

Rome's struggle with the Samnites for ascendancy in Central Italy was protracted through three wars, the first beginning in 343 B.C., the last ending in 290 B.C. At the battle of the Caudine Forks, an entire army of Romans was forced to capitulate. So late as the time of Sulla, the Samnites attempted unsuccessfully to throw off the yoke of Rome. — **non Poeni**: especially, of course, in the conflict with Hannibal, 218–201 B.C. — **Hispaniae**: the subjugation of Spain, to which Rome acquired the title after the Second Punic War, was marked by a long series of disasters to the Roman arms; the reverses were due alike to the determined opposition of the Lusitanians under the brave and able leadership of Viriathus, and to the incapacity and knavery of the Roman commanders. The capture of Numantia by Scipio Aemilianus in 133 B.C. ended the resistance of the natives. — **Galliae**: in the invasion of the Senones, 390–387 B.C., marked by the annihilation of a Roman army at the Allia and by the siege of the Capitol, and in subsequent forays of the Celts in 360 and 348 B.C. Gallic wars in 238–222 B.C. ended in the occupation of Cisalpine Gaul by the Romans. The uprising of the Gauls under Vercingetorix was the most serious crisis in Caesar's conquest of Transalpine Gaul.

13. Parthi: the ill-fated expedition of Crassus, which came to grief in 53 B.C., and the abortive ending of Antony's attempt at an invasion of Parthia in 36 B.C., are the outstanding features of the continued disputes between Rome and the Parthians for the possession of Syria and Armenia, and the control of the East. The return (20 B.C.) of the standards captured from Crassus marked only a lull in the protracted clash of interests between these two traditional foes. — **Arsăcis**: founder and first monarch of the Parthian Empire who, about 250 B.C., brought about the secession of the Parthians from the rule of the Seleucids. His name was assumed as a title by his successors; cf. the analogous history of the name Caesar.

14. acrior: *a sharper stimulus.* Even in the monarchical states the Germans enjoyed a fuller measure of popular freedom than obtained in the Oriental despotism.

15. et ipse: as in A*gricola* 25. 22, *diviso et ipse in tris partis exercitu incessit,* emphasizing a supplementary fact or consideration; translate: *the East on its part.* — **Pacŏro**: son of Orodes I and commander of the Parthian armies in several unsuccessful invasions of Syria, the last of which, in 38 B.C., ended in the complete defeat of Pacorus and his death in battle. Thus the deaths of two conspicuous leaders, one on each side, offset each other. — infra **Ventidium deiectus Oriens**: the personification is similar to that contained in the lines from Halleck's *Marco Bozzaris:*

> " The Turk was dreaming of the hour
> When Greece, her knees in suppliance bent,
> Should tremble at his power."

Abasement at the feet of a Ventidius was insult added to injury, insinuates Tacitus, breathing the scorn of the aristocrat for the upstart. P. Ventidius Bassus, consul suffectus 43 B.C., legate of Antony and conqueror of Pacorus, had risen from a lowly origin, having, so scandal asserted, once been a muleteer.

16. Carbone: Papirius Carbo, consul in 113 B.C., mentioned above. He treacherously attacked the Cimbri, though they had complied with his orders to withdraw from the territory of the Taurisci, and was defeated. A storm alone saved his army from utter destruction.

17. Cassio: in 107 B.C., L. Cassius Longinus, the consul, was killed and his army cut down or captured by the Tigurini, a Helvetian people which, as an incident to the great tribal movements of the time, made common cause with the Cimbri and pressed into Southern Gaul. — **Scauro . . . Caepione . . . Mallio**: consular legate, proconsul, and consul respectively, commanders of the Roman armies which in 105 B.C. essayed to oppose at the Rhone the advance of the Cimbri toward Italy. The battle of Arausio, which ensued, ended in a disaster to Roman arms "which materially and morally surpassed the day of Cannae" (Mommsen). *Caepione* and *Mallio* are joined closely, apart from *Scauro*, because his detachment was cut to pieces and he himself captured in an engagement separate from the battle proper.

18. quinque : for the sake of making as strong a case as possible, Tacitus has committed a slight exaggeration ; Carbo's army suffered a reverse but was not destroyed. Another defeat which Tacitus might have added to his catalogue was that inflicted on M. Innius Silanus and his army in 109 B.C.

20. **Caesari abstulerunt**: for, under the Empire, the princeps was *de jure* commander-in-chief of the armies and expeditions were carried out under his auspices. In connection with *abstulerunt* we may compare the wail of Augustus, Suetonius, *Augustus* 23 : *Quintili Vare, legiones* redde. — **Marius in Italia**: of the two great victories, one at Aquae Sextiae in Gaul (102 B.C.) and the other at Vercellae near the *Po* (101 B.C.), by which Italy was saved for the time being from conquest by the Germans, the latter only is mentioned, doubtless because it was the final and decisive engagement.

21. **Iulius in Gallia**: the victory over Ariovistus in 58 B.C. and the rout of the Usipetes and the Tencteri in 55 B.C., are instances in point. — Nero: *i.e.* Tiberius.

22. ingentes **Gai Caesaris** minae: Caligula's expedition of 39 A.D., referred to in *Agricola*, 13. 11 f.: *ni . . . ingentes adversus Germaniam conatus frustra fuissent.* As has been pointed out in the note on this passage of the *Agricola*, the actual achievements of the campaign were out of keeping with its pretensions, though as a military demonstration it may not have been entirely futile. We may be sure that Caligula's acts lost nothing of the picturesque in the accounts given of him by the ancient historians.

24. occasione . . **civilium armorum**: coincident with the civil wars of 69 A.D., the "Year of the Four Emperors," was the insurrection of the Batavi under the leadership of Civilis; the revolt was undertaken ostensibly to further the cause of Vespasian against Vitellius, but was continued after the former had made good his claim to the principate.

26. proximis temporibus triumphati: an allusion to the so-called *falsus e Germania triumphus* (*Agricola* 39. 4), cele-

brated by Domitian after his campaign against the Chatti in
83–84 A.D. The extension and fortification of the frontier were
tangible and significant results of his operations, which, however, in the eyes of his critics, did not justify a triumph.

Chapter **38.**

The Suebian races; their characteristic national head-dress.

1. nunc de **Suebis**: the account of the peoples gathered by
Tacitus under the generic term *Suebi* is continued through
chap. 45. From the information here given, the sources of
which it is impossible to fix, it would appear that the name was
applied to a confederation of separate, though cognate, races,
united in the worship of a common divinity. Their original
habitat, bounded on the west by the Elbe, extended far to the
east and northeast, whence it is that the Baltic could be called
Suebicum Mare (chap. 45). Their adventurous and aggressive
temperament led to constant expansion of their domination,
mentioned by Caesar, *Bellum Gallicum* 4. 3, as a national am-
bitiou. Large bodies of them had migrated from their native
haunts before the time of Caesar and had established themselves in Southern and Southwestern Germany. Here they
made such races as the Usipetes, Tencteri, and Ubii chronic
victims of their " will to power," and ultimately became known
to Caesar as *gens longe maxima et bellicosissima Germanorum
omnium.*

The name, in all probability originating in non-Suebian peoples
and having the general force of an epithet, was easily extensible
and naturally as applicable to any one of the races of the confederation as their ethnic name proper. Furthermore, the rapid
growth of Suebian power doubtless caused confusion between
the true Suebi and races which had come under their sphere
of influence. These considerations help to explain the variation of the application of the name discernible in the ancient
sources. The term, as utilized by Tacitus in chap. 2, is com-
posite but is restricted to true Suebian stocks which had occupied
territory west and south of the Elbe, being set off from the
peoples of Eastern Germany, embraced under the name Vandilii.
(See notes on 2. 16.) The extension of the name in this and the

following chapters, to include all the peoples of Eastern Germany between the Danube and the Baltic, the Suiones of the Scandinavian Peninsula, and even some non-Germanic races, transcends all limits of usage elsewhere and rests upon a different set of data from that utilized in chap. 2.

3. adhuc: *besides, i.e.* in addition to the collective name Suebi.

5. obliquare **crinem**: *to comb the hair athwart* (from its natural direction or 'hang'). The locks thus arranged lay *across* or *at an angle* with the perpendicular lines in which they would have hung had they been combed down. — nodo . . . **sub-** stringere : the position of the knot on the head was subject to variation, as we might surmise and as is evident from line 11 below. In certain artistic representations of ancient Germans the knot is to be seen on one side of the head, over the ear.

6. Suebi a ceteris **Germanis**: according to the testimony of Tacitus, this style of dressing the hair would be widespread among the Germans and would have especially attracted the observation of the Romans. Naturally, therefore, as is evident from references in other writers of the Empire, the n*odus* came to be regarded as the distinctive racial coiffure of all Germans.

8. imitatione: as the fashionable youths of Athens are said to have worn their hair long in imitation of the Spartan mode; see Lysias, 'Υπὲρ Μαντιθέου 18; Aristophanes, *Equites* 580.

9. rarum: sc. *est*.

10. usque **ad canitiem**: balances *intra iuventae spatium*. No member contrasting with *rarum* is expressed because the fashion has been characterized as common to the whole body of Suebian freemen. — retro sequuntur: the locution is surprising; perhaps the image present in the mind of the writer is the movement of the comb back from the forehead in the process of arrangement.

11. ornatiorem: *a more elaborate arrangement;* sc. *capillum.*

12. ut ament amenturve: a shaft directed at the fop and débauché of Roman society. A too punctilious arrangement of the hair was proverbially a mark of effeminacy; see, *e.g.,* the biting epigram of Calvus on Pompey, *Magnus quem metuunt omnes, digito caput uno scalpit*, et seq. (' Magnus, of whom all are in awe, scratches his head with one finger '; Müller, *Frag-menta*, p. 86, no. 18); Cicero, *Pro Sestio* 8. 18–19, the contrast between the young profligate *unguentis adfluens, calamistrata coma* (' dripping with perfumes, with locks curled by the iron '), and the type of old-time Roman *capillo ita horrido; Catiline,* 2. sect. 22 (of Catiline's partisans), *quos pexo capillo, nitidos . . videtis.*

13. in . . . altitudinem quandam: there is an ellipsis of an adversative idea before the preposition, which is used in its frequent final sense, *with a view to.* The phrase is joined closely to *compti.*

14. ut hostium oculis armantur: this is the .elliptical use of *ut,* to limit an assertion to particular conditions or circumstances, which is to be seen in such contexts as Livy, 4. 13. 1: *Spurius Maelius . ut illis temporibus, praedives* (' Spurius Maelius . . . for those times a very rich man '); Cicero, *Brutus* 10. 41: *Themistocles . . . ut apud nos, perantiquus; ut apud Athenienses, non ita sane vetus* (' Themistocles . . . as judged by our stand-ards, belonging to a very early age — as judged by Athenian standards, not of such an ancient epoch '); cf. also *Germania,* 30. 7. Translate: *they are armed, — for the eyes of the enemy that is* (not, of course, for the give-and-take of physical combat for which they need other weapons than an awe-inspiring ap-pearance).

The influence of ocular impressions on the issue of battle is a rhetorical commonplace; cf. ·Gorgias, *Encomium of Helen* 16; in Xenophon, *Symposium* 2. 14, the coward Pisander, the Athenian Bob Acres, does not enlist διὰ τὸ μὴ δύνασθαι λόγχαις ἀντιβλέπειν (' by reason of inability to stand the sight of spears '); Propertius, 4. 6. 49–50; Tacitus, *Agricola* 32. 14 f., and *Germania* 43. 25.

Chapter 39.

The Semnŏnes; the central cult of the Suebi.

1. nobilissimos: cf. the similar claim made by Calgacus, *Agricola* 30. 10, *nobilissimi totius Britanniae.* — **Semnŏnes**: they occupied at this time the territory between the Elbe and the Oder of which the Duchy of Brandenburg is now a part.

In later times, they were merged with other races under the appellation Alamanni; however, they did not lose their original ethnic identity as Suebi, for it is from them that modern Suabia, once a part of the domain of the Alamanni, received its name.

2. stato tempore: *at a standing festal season*, not necessarily of annual recurrence.

3. silvam . . . sacram: cf. 9. 9, *lucos ac nemora consecrant.* — auguriis patrum et prisca formidine sacram: these words form a complete hexameter. Tacitus doubtless slipped into the rhythm unconsciously; similar lapses — for so ancient stylists considered them — occur semi-occasionally elsewhere in Latin prose writers. The first clause in Livy's preface to his history forms part of a hexameter and in Book 22. 50 the words *haec ubi dicta dedit, stringit gladium cuneoque facto per medios* are a hexameter and a half. The diction here has a poetic color, comparable to Vergil, Aeneid 7. 172, *(tectum) horrendum silvis et religione parentum*, and this fact rendered it easy for Tacitus to glide into a rhythmic cadence. The ablatives are causal; translate: *owing to portents which appeared to their sires*, et cet.

4. eiusdem sanguinis: i.e. *Sueborum.*

5. publice: *in the name of the association.* On human sacrifice among the Germans, see note on 9. 2.

6. horrenda primordia: *gruesome introductory ceremonies.*

7. nisi vinculo ligatus: the interpretation given by Tacitus of the inner significance of this usage is correct. Cords and bonds figure not infrequently in ritual and religion as symbols of the subjection of a devotee to a deity. The fillet used in Greek and Roman worship was in origin a badge of devotion and consecration to a higher power. See on the subject, Bonner, *The Sacred Bond, American Philological Association, Transactions and Proceedings*, 44 (1913), esp. p. 239. — minor: *an inferior;* cf. Horace, *Epistulae* 1. 1. 106, *sapiens uno minor est Iove* (' the philosopher is inferior to Jove alone ')·

8. prae se ferens: *giving open testimony to.* Cf. Agricola 43. 14, *speciem doloris . . . prae se tulit.* — attolli: reflexive in meaning, as is also *evolvuntur* below. The notion underlying the observance was doubtless that a fall was due to the visitation of providence and that he whom the god had cast down could not, without defying the divine will, raise himself to his feet while within the limits of the precinct.

10. superstitio: not to be translated by the English derivative. It was the term applied by the Romans to any barbarian cult that had not received the sanction of the state religion. The word had somewhat the same connotation to the Roman as heathenism has to the Christian. — **tamquam**: *sint* is to be supplied. — **initia gentis**: the god to whom the grove was sacred was regarded as the progenitor of the Suebi, his precinct as the " cradle of the race." The claim of the Semnones to be the original Suebi and the " chosen people," rested on the fact that the grove was in their land and under their custody.

11. deus: this supreme divinity of the Suebi was, in all probability, Tiu.

12. centum pagi: Caesar, *Bellum Gallicum* 4. 1. 4, makes a similar assertion concerning the Suebi of Southwest Germany.

13. magno . . . corpore: referring to the numerical preponderance of the " body politic."

Chapter 40.

The Langobardi; the seven tribes that worshiped the goddess Nerthus; her cult.

1. Langobardos: the forefathers of the powerful Lombards who, in 568 A.D., under the command of Alboin, invaded Italy. Some critics believe that the Langobardi had their seat originally in Scandinavia, whence they emigrated to Germany. However this may be, we find them in Roman times established along the lower Elbe, south and southeast of modern Hamburg. —**plurimis ac valentissimis nationibus**: such as the Chauci to the north and west, the Angrivarii to the west, the Dulgubnii and the Semnones on the south and southeast.

3. proeliis ac periclitando: editors quote in this connection the comment of Velleius Paterculus, 2. 106, who, writing in the principate of Tiberius, characterizes this race as *etiam Germana feritate ferocior*. We should temper this statement by recalling that the history of Velleius is encomiastic and that he was concerned to magnify the deeds of his hero, Tiberius, against the Langobardi. The topical form of the comment betrays its rhetorical nature ; cf. the locution of the same type in Livy, 21. 4, *perfidia* (*Hannibalis*) *plus quam Punica.* — **deinde :** *next in position*, *i.e.* to the north, since Tacitus in his description proceeds from the interior to the sea.

The tribes here named, united in a cult group, were located north of the Elbe, in the vicinity of Hamburg and Lübeck, and still farther to the north in Schleswig-Holstein. The Anglii or Angles, the later invaders of Britain, may be definitely placed along the east coast of Schleswig, north of the Kiel canal. The neighboring Varīni were closely related to them.

6. in commune : they are united in a cult association. — **Nerthum :** closely analogous to the rites of Nerthus here described were those celebrated in Rome, during the Empire, in honor of Magna Mater or Cybele. A feature of the festival of Magna Mater was the *lavatio*, performed on March 27 of each year ; the cult symbol of the goddess, the famous meteorite brought from Phrygia in 205 B.C., was placed on a car drawn by cows, and was escorted by a procession to a small tributary of the Tiber, the Almo. The idol, the chariot, and the other paraphernalia of the cult underwent a ceremonial lustration in the waters of the brook.

It seems probable, therefore, that, after the fashion of the Roman student of comparative religion (see also note on 3. 1), Tacitus has identified Nerthus with Magna Mater on the basis of these striking external resemblances in cult rites and did not possess any accurate information as to the essential nature of the German goddess. She is commonly regarded as the feminine counterpart of a male divinity, Njördr, worshiped by the Norse peoples as a god of fertility, the weather, and trade.

7. Terram matrem : stress has been laid on the fact that Nerthus is defined, not as *Magna* Mater but as *Terra* Mater ; hence the theory has been advanced that Tacitus intended that his readers should regard her, not as the German Cybele, but as a goddess of the earth and vegetation, comparable to the Roman Tellus (also Terra) Mater, whose festival was celebrated on April 15 and who stood in close connection with the Manes as a divinity of the lower world ; see, *e.g.*, Suetonius, *Tiberius* 85. This view, however, presupposes a ritualistic precision in the language of Tacitus which seems unlikely in the face of the tendency, constantly visible in Roman mythology and religion, to blend the personalities and the functions of Ops, Terra, Magna Mater, Ceres, et cet.—intervenire : *mingles in.*

8. invehi populis : *populis* is dative. The image of the goddess, we are to understand, was drawn from place to place ; cf. the allusion in Tibullus, 1. 4. 68-9, to the similar progress of the car of Cybele, escorted by her priests :

> *Idaeae currus ille sequatur Opis*
> *et tercentenas erroribus expleat urbes*

(' let him follow the cars of Idaean Ops and complete the tale of thrice a hundred cities in his wanderings '). — **insula Oceani :** an old but erroneous folk tradition settled on Rügen, off the coast of Pomerania, in the Baltic, as the sacred isle and furnished it with a Lake Hertha, a name derived from a manuscript corruption of *Nerthus* (cf. the similar origin of " Grampian " from a mistaken reading *Grampius* for *Graupius* in *Agricola* 29. 8). Later scholarship, with an enthusiasm pardonable but barren of results, has advanced the claims of other islands both in the Baltic and the North Sea. — **castum** nemus : the grove was kept unviolated by mortal tread ; cf. Ovid, Fasti 4. 751, the prayer of the shepherd to Pales : *Si nemus intravi vetitum*
> *da veniam culpae* (' If I have entered a forbidden grove, grant mercy to my fault ').

9. veste : *a trapping of cloth.*

10. penetrali : the wagon is the ark of the goddess. .

11. bubus feminis : the chariot of Magna Mater was also drawn by cows.

12. quaecumque . . . dignatur : it has been assumed by a recent critic that, because the center of the cult of Nerthus was on an island, the whole ceremonial was necessarily confined to the one district and that large deputations, the *populi* referred to above, were sent by the participating states and es⁻tablished themselves in separate camps around the sacred grove. Even though Tacitus does not say how the goddess and her car were transported to the mainland, his language certainly makes for the view that they were. *Populi* can hardly mean *legationes populorum* (cf. 39. 4) and *quaecumque . . . dignatur* points to an extended itinerary as does also the analogy furnished by similar progresses from place to place of wagons, ships on wheels, and the like on festive occasions in later ages.

13. non bella ineunt: such truces often accompanied interstate religious festivals; cf. the ἐκεχειρία, or 'sacred armistice' proclaimed for the month in which the Olympic Games were celebrated. A similar "truce of God" was observed during the period of the *Feriae Latinae*, the common festival of the Latins held in honor of Jupiter Latiaris on the Alban Mt.

16. templo: not a building (cf. note on 9. 7), but the holy precinct.

18. numen ipsum: the conviction of the devotees was that not an image but the goddess herself was bathed; otherwise the clause *si credere velis* would not have been evoked, cognizant as Tacitus and his generation were of the *lavatio* of the cult symbol of Magna Mater. An analogous rite was performed by women on the statue of Venus Verticordia on April 1; cf. Ovid, *Fasti* 4. 136. Instances of the lustration of cult statues were not uncommon in Greek rituals; *e.g.* the xoanon of Athene was bathed at Athens on the occasion of the festival of the *Plynteria;* in the tragedy of Euripides, *Iphigenia among the Taurians*, the stratagem by which Iphigenia steals the image of Artemis and makes good the escape of Orestes, Pylades, and herself from King Thoas, centers about a feigned intent to purify the statue by bathing it in the sea.

19. quos . . . haurit: the story of Actaeon is perhaps a mythical expression of the feeling underlying the German rite, viz. that he to whom the person of a goddess has been revealed unveiled should not live to tell the tale. Or the destruction of the ministrants may have been conceived of frankly as a human sacrifice. — **arcanus:** *mysterious.*

Chapter **41.**

The Hermundŭri and their relations with Rome.

1. secretiora: *more remote* from the *limes.*

3. nunc Danuvium sequar: he proceeds from west to east in his narrative. — **Hermundurorum:** eastern neighbors of the

Chatti; their lands extended north to the Hartz Mts. and east to the Elbe, thus embracing the Saxon Duchies and Southern Saxony. They figure in later history as the Thuringi.

4. in ripa: of the Danube. Their territory did not extend to the river but they were allowed free access to it for purposes of trade.

5. penitus: said from the point of view of the Hermunduri, who were permitted to pass into Roman territory.

6. colonia: *Augusta Vindelicorum*, situated somewhat north of the modern Augsburg, and founded as a market town by Drusus in 15 B.C. The place did not, in the time of Trajan, have technically the standing of a *colonia*, hence Tacitus has used the term here in a free, not a formal, sense. — **passim et sine custode**: the *limes* ordinarily formed a customs-barrier which rigorously controlled the entry of the Germans even when bound on peaceful errands; passage was allowed at specified places only, the incoming barbarian had to pay a fee and to submit to disarmament and surveillance.

8. domos villasque: they were allowed access to town- and country-houses alike.

9. Albis oritur: the domains of the Hermunduri certainly did not embrace Bohemia, where the Elbe takes its rise. Either Tacitus was under the impression that the source of the river was in the Erzgebirge between Saxony and Bohemia, or he mistook the Saale, a tributary of the Elbe, for the Elbe proper.

10. notum olim: Drusus and Tiberius had penetrated to the Elbe and, in 2 B.C., L. Domitius Ahenobarbus had operated on the eastern bank. In 17 A.D. Germanicus, after his recall from Germany, celebrated a triumph over the Cherusci, the Chatti, the Angrivarii, and 'the other nations which extend as far as the Elbe,' with more *réclame*, however, than his conquests justified. — **nunc . . . auditur**: because, with the recall of Germanicus by Tiberius, the policy of wide expansion in Germany had been relinquished.

Chapter 42.

The Naristi, the Marcomanni, and the Quadi.

1. Naristi: they lived east of the Hermunduri, in what is now Northeastern Bavaria. — **Marcomani**: *i.e.* 'Border-men,' cf. modern German *Mark*, ' boundary.' Since the last decade B.C., they had occupied Bohemia, where, under the leadership of their king, Marobod, they formed the nucleus of a powerful confederacy. Their supremacy was ended for the time being when King Marobod was defeated in a war with the Cherusci, begun in 17 A.D., was abandoned by his allies, and forced to take refuge in Italy. The second century A.D. witnessed a renascence of their power and, in a series of wars with Rome in the time of Marcus Aurelius, they were put down only after a stubborn contest.

2. Quadi: akin to the Marcomanni and closely united with their history during the first two centuries of the Empire. Their territory was the modern Moravia.

3. pulsis olim Boiis: the fact that the great mass of the Boii had left their original seats and been dispersed in various lands in the west and the south some years prior to the time of Caesar's campaigns in Gaul, whereas the Marcomanni under Marobod did not settle in Bohemia until the close of the century, has caused the accuracy of this assertion to be questioned. However, bands of the Marcomanni, abandoning their former abode between the Main and the Danube, had established themselves in Bohemia during the period of the emigrations of the Boii. These earlier incursions had at least paved the way for the occupation of the territory by Marobod, and it is possible that remnants of the Boii that still maintained a foothold offered a futile resistance to him.

5. velut frons: these tribes are thought of as facing Rome. **— peragitur:** *is constituted by;* a different region, of course, would be *frons Germaniae* where the Rhine formed the boundary.

7. Tudri: mentioned here only.

8. iam et externos: as *iam* indicates, recent events are here referred to, but we are ignorant as to the details of the change in dynasty.

10. nec minus: their position is maintained as effectively by financial aid as by armed intervention; cf. 15. 12, *iam et pecuniam accipere docuimus.*

Chapter **43**.

The East Germans.

1. retro: north and east. The point of view is the
as that implied in *velut frons*, 42. 5.   The four tribes her
tioned, inhabiting a country for the most part mount:
were, therefore, located in and near the Riesengebirge a
Western Carpathians.   The Buri lived in the vicinity of r
Cracow, the Cotini on the Upper Gran, the Osi, also refei
in 28. 10 f., in Northwestern Hungary, north of the grea
of the Danube.

3. referunt: *reproduce.* — **Cotïnos Gallica:** the Cotin
undoubtedly a survival of the Celtic tribes which, mainly g
under the collective name Boii, were in possession of the
north of the Danube at the time of the great migration
Cimbri.

5. Sarmătae: the Iazyges, a Sarmatian tribe living b
the Danube and the Theiss.

6. quo magis pudeat: to heighten their disgrace, they
to exactions, although they have at their disposal mater
fashioning weapons with which to assert their independenc

9. continuum . . . **iugum:** the watershed formed b
Erzgebirge, the Riesengebirge, the Sudetics, and continued
east by the Carpathians.

10. ultra quod: to the north.

11. Lygiorum: Lygii and Vandilii were both collective 1
each of which comprehended a number of the peoples o
Germany; the names existed for a time side by side and v
some extent interchangeable until, in later times, the
name gained exclusive currency in the derived form *Van*

The several tribes of the Lygian confederacy, which ar
listed, occupied the country now comprised by Silesia,
and Poland, the Vistula forming their eastern boundary.

14. antiquae religionis lucus: the cult center of the
union, comparable to the grove of the Semnones, 39. 3.

15. sacerdos muliebri ornatu: he was dressed in f
robes and wore his hair arranged in the feminine mode.
the fact that the name of the royal line of the Vandals,
d*ng*i, signifies ' men with women's coiffure,' it has been pla

conjectured that, as was the case in the primitive Greco-Roman kingship, the functions of monarch and priest were united in the ruling house of these eastern tribes.

16. vis: *the inherent character.*

17. Alcis: regarded by most critics as a dative plural; however, neither this point nor the identity of the divine pair itself has been absolutely demonstrated. — **peregrinae superstitionis:** the cult was indigenous, not imported as was, according to Tacitus, the worship of Isis, alluded to in chap. 9; cf. 9. 4, *peregrino sacro,* et seq.

18. tamen: notwithstanding the lack of concrete data making for the identification of these deities with Castor and Pollux, their divine personality conforms with that of the Twin Brethren.

19. ceterum: indicating a return to the description of the people after the digression concerning the cult; for a like usage see A*gricola* 11. 1. — **super:** = *praeter.*

21. arte ac tempore: itemized below. — **lenocinantur:** *they heighten, promote.*

22. tincta: by application of a black pigment or "war-paint" before going into battle. The Britons resorted to a more durable, vegetable dye for a similar purpose; cf. Caesar, *Bellum Gallicum* 5. 14: *omnes vero se Britanni vitro inficiunt quod caeruleum efficit colorem atque hoc horribiliores sunt in pugna aspectu.* — **ipsa . . . formidine . . . exercitus:** *by the sheer dread inspired by the shadowy appearance of their unearthly host.*

24. novum: *weird.*

25. primi . . . oculi vincuntur: on this sentiment see note on 38. 14.

27. Gotōnes: the Goths. This famous race, destined to play so great a rôle in the future history of the Roman world, lived at this time north of the Lygii along the lower Vistula. By the third century A.D., as the result of a series of folk-movements, they had established a powerful kingdom in Southern Russia. — **regnantur:** the ideas of location and government are blended in the one word; as we might put it — ' is situated the kingdom of the Goths.' — **adductius:** the metaphor may be reproduced by some such rendition as, *the reins of government being drawn more tightly.*

28. supra libertatem: the monarchical form was not
potic as to have abolished the popular freedom typical of
man states.

29. Rugii et Lemovii: on the shore of the Baltic betw
Oder and the Vistula.

30. rotunda scuta, breves gladii: that arms of these
were, as Tacitus says, characteristic of the equipment of t
Germans is amply demonstrated by the finds made in
notably in West Prussia. Here numerous bosses have b
covered, which evidently were once attached to round
and a type of short, iron sword, resembling a saber and e
one side only. Arms of these types were occasionally in us
tribes dwelling west of the Oder, the Suebi, for exampl
illustrations see F. Kauffmann, *Deutsche Altertumskunde*
Plates 27. 3–5 and 34. 3.

Chapter 44.

The Suiǒnes.

1. Suiǒnum: the Latinized form of the ancient Swedi
of the inhabitants of the Scandinavian Peninsula; the
term ' Swede ' is a derivative of the original root. — hi
point of view is the coast between the Oder and the Vis
ipso in Oceano: Scandinavia was regarded as an immens

2. classibus valent: thus the later vikings came natu
their nautical skill and daring. — **differt**: from Roman

3. utrimque prora: the adverb is used attributivel
shape of such boats was similar to that of the modern ca
whaleboat. Craft of this type were constructed by Gerᵢ
for use in his expedition to the North Sea in 16 A.D.; cf.
scription in *Annales* 2. 6: *plures (naves) adpositis utrimque ᵩ
culis, converso ut repente remigio hinc vel illinc adpeller*
number of the ships were equipped with steering gear
ends that, by a sudden shift of the oars, they might pᵢ
shore either way '). They were especially suited to the
tion of rivers and narrow fiords where " sea-room " for
might be lacking.

4. nec . . . in ordinem: the boats were not rigged ᵴ
have the oars in a permanent, fixed arrangement, symᵣ

on each side in respect to number of sweeps and intervals apart, as was the case with Roman galleys.

5. solutum: *detachable.* — **in quibusdam fluminum**: a stylistic variant of *in . . . fluminibus.*

7. opibus: *wealth.* — unus **imperitat**: an inference which would naturally be suggested to a Roman by the traditional combination of riches and absolutism in the persons of the Oriental despots; see as a typical illustration Phraates, Horace, *Odes* 2. 2. 16 f. The proverbial point of view of the Roman is expressed by Milton, *Paradise Lost* 2. 3:

> " Or where the gorgeous East with richest hand
> Showers on her kings barbaric pearl and gold."

— nullis iam **exceptionibus**: *in this instance without limitations; iam* implies a contrast with the more or less restricted power wielded generally by the German kings.

8. non precario iure **parendi**: *with a claim on obedience not subject to approval,* on the part of his constituency, as it were.

9. clausa sub custode: it has been suggested that Tacitus here erroneously reports as a standing condition of affairs what was only a temporary disarmament, enforced during a sacred truce which accompanied the celebration of a religious festival; cf. the similar custom among the worshipers of Nerthus, chap. 40. Disarmament of the subject population was a traditional device of the ancient Greek tyranny, and it was naturally from this point of view that an ancient writer might interpret the practice elsewhere. Recall the disarmament of the Athenians by the Thirty (Xenophon, *Hellenica* 2. 3. 20) and the stratagem (perhaps apocryphal, Busolt, 2. p. 34. note 2) by which Pisistratus secured the weapons of the citizens ; Aristotle, *Constitution of Athens* 15. 4.

11. manus: best taken literally — ". Satan findeth mischief still for idle hands to do "

Chapter 45.

The inert Northern Ocean; the Aestii and their goddess; amber; the Sitŏnes.

1. aliud **mare**: distinct from *Oceanus,* the term applied to the seas adjacent to the German coast, the North Sea or the Baltic

128 NOTES

according to the context. **pigrum ac** prope **inmotum**: th(
qualities, density and lack of mobility, are ascribed in A;
10. 20 to the waters about Thule ; see the note on this pa

2. hinc: anticipating the evidence contained in the foll
quod clause. It should be remembered in this context th
explanation of the cause of the Midnight Sun as given in A;
12. 14, *scilicet extrema et plana terrarum humili umbra non ε
tenebras*, assumes that the phenomenon is visible only ;
edge of the world.

· **5. radios capitis**: a regular feature of literary and a
portrayals of the Sun God ; he even places them on the h(
Phaethon before the fatal course, Ovid, *Metamorphoses 2
Cf. Vergil's description of the crown of Latinus, *Aeneid* 12. 1

> . . . *cui tempora circum
> aurati bis sex radii fulgentia cingunt,
> Solis avi specimen.* . . .

— persuasio*: *popular belief*. It can scarcely be to op
actually current among the peoples of the far North to
Tacitus alludes. The notions here referred to accord so evi(
with the conception of the Sun God as we find it in Greco-R
mythology, that it is a fair inference that Tacitus is repeat
a deprecatory tone statements found in literary sources, R
or more probably Hellenistic ; at least such naïve ideas of n;
phenomena suggest the age and manner of Pytheas, the '
traveler who, in the second half of the fourth century
reported to the civilized world the existence of the coagi
sea, or even of the Stoic philosopher, Posidonius, Cicero's
contemporary, who asserted that the sun, when it dropped
Western Ocean, hissed like a mass of red-hot iron.

Note that Tacitus does not assume responsibility for th(
in this sentence, whereas, in those which precede and f
fides and *fama vera* respectively show that he vouches f(
truth of his assertions.

6. tantum natura: the meaning of *natura* here, ' the n
world,' ' creation,' is the same as in *Agricola* 33. 28. T
may have believed his confident assertion justified by his l
edge of the information gained by Agricola's expediti

exploration. — ergo iam : the connection is : since this northern region marks the end of the known world and there is nothing more to be said concerning this locality, I turn accordingly at this point to the east coast of the Baltic.

7. Aestiorum gentes : the peoples who dwelt along the Baltic, in East Prussia and Russia as far as the Gulf of Finland. They were non-Germanic in origin and were the ancestors of the Old Prussians, Lithuanians, and Letts. It is supposed that the modern Esthonians, though of Finnish stock, have perpetuated the name.

8. lingua Britannicae propior : the ears of unscientific observers, probably traders, detected in the language of the Aestii sounds which bore a certain resemblance to the more familiar Celtic. Similarly, in *Agricola* 11. 12, Tacitus cites the resemblance between the languages of the Gauls and the southeast Britons as an indication that the latter were of Gallic extraction. However, neither Tacitus nor the ancient world in general had anything but a rudimentary conception of the utilization of linguistic criteria in the differentiation of races.

9. matrem deum : the data are too meager to justify our assuming on the basis of this context the actual existence among these peoples of the cult of a mother goddess. Figures of boars were worn as amulets by the devotees of Magna Mater in Rome and similar insignia, seen on the natives of the East Baltic coast, may have without further reason inspired the theory.

10. omnium : neuter. The genitive is objective.

Belief in the efficacy of inanimate objects to protect the bearer from harm, emanating from natural or supernatural sources, is ages old and still finds expression in modern times, *e.g.* in the Italian's faith in his coral prophylactic against the evil eye. The superstition has never been confined to one race or branch of mankind. In Northern Europe graves, dating back to the Stone and Bronze Ages, have yielded amulets of many types and fashioned from many materials, such as stone, horn, shell, the teeth, bones, and claws (cf. ' the rabbit's foot ' of Negro superstition) of various animals.

14. laborant : in Augustan poetry, the accusative follows *laborāre* to denote the thing wrought out or produced by work.

K

Here *they take pains in cultivating* is an approximate rendit: sed **et**: they do not confine themselves to the land in the of a livelihood, *but*, et seq. — omnium : i.e. *Germanorum.*

15. glesum: English *glass*, *glare*, German *Glanz*, *glänz* from the root which appears in this word. — **inter vada at** ipso litore : from the Stone Age to the present day the Pr coast has been famed for its amber. In the time of T Samland, north of Königsberg in East Prussia, had practic monopoly of this commodity and is still the chief source world's supply ; Dantzig is the principal depot of the trad

Amber is still gathered on the coast by searchers wl equipped with nets attached to long poles, and who ransa shallows at low tide. Dredging operations and divers ar employed. Amber is likewise found in pit deposits at distance from the sea and is in this case obtained by n processes.

17. ut barbaris: *as would naturally be the case among rians*; cf. *Agricola* 11. 2, *ut inter barbaros.*

18. luxuria nostra : as a matter of fact, however, ambe prized at very early periods of civilization. In the Ston amber ornaments were the favorite articles of personal adorn as the graves of the period testify. In the Bronze Age { ceased to be so highly favored among the northern peoples had learned to know bronze and gold, but it became an { of commerce and was spread by various trade routes Mediterranean and Western Europe, where it was eagerly comed. Objects of amber have been found in the Myce tombs of Greece, in the lake dwellings of Italy, and even a relics of the Bronze Age in England.

Of these facts Tacitus, of course, had no knowledge, s(fines himself to mentioning amber as an article of Roman lt in which it began to have a place in the late Republic ar early Empire. Great quantities of it were brought to Ro the principate of Nero to be used in enhancing the magnif of a gladiatorial exhibition ; cf. Pliny, *Naturalis Historia* 11. 45. The substance was used chiefly in the manufactu necklaces and other articles of feminine adornment ; s hilts, utensils of various sorts, and statuettes were fash from it, and it was also esteemed for certain medicinal qualities which it was supposed to possess.

19. nomen : *reputation.*

20. profertur : *is offered for sale.* — sucum **arborum :** in modern scientific parlance, *fossilized resin.*

21. terrena . . . volucria animalia : an assertion completely verified by modern observation ; among the inclosures have been found remains of insects, worms, crustaceans, occasional fragments of hair and feathers, and also leaves and plant structures.

See Herrick " On a Fly buried in Amber," a theme imported into poetry by Martial, 4. 32 ; cf. Bacon, *Sylva Sylvarum, Century I. Experiment* 100 : " We see how flies, and spiders, and the like, get a sepulchre in amber, more durable than the monument and embalming of the body of any king," and Pope, *Epistle to* Dr. A*rbuthnot* 169 :

" Pretty in amber to observe the forms
Of hairs, or straws, or dirt, or grubs, or worms."

24. fecundiora : the comparative denotes the possession of the quality in an unwonted degree.

26. quae : the connection is rendered hazy by the fact that the antecedent is not expressed but was felt to be implied by the substances involved in *fecundiora;* translate : *Just as in out-of-the-way corners of the Orient, where frankincense and balsam are distilled (from the trees), so . . . there are forests and groves teeming to an unusual degree (with substances) which,* et cet.

29. in modum taedae : it is reported — the editor cannot personally vouch for the facts — that at the present time the rough fragments of amber which are cast up on the west coast of Schleswig-Holstein are utilized by the poorer classes for light ; cf. the name *Bernstein* (*Brennstein*).

30. in . . . lentescit : *it turns into a viscous substance resembling,* et cet.

32. Sitŏnum gentes : it is conjectured that they were Finnish tribes who occupied the northern part of Scandinavia. To classify them with the Suebi is an ethnological error pure and simple. — continuantur : *are next to.*

33. femina dominatur: probably a myth and perhaps founded on a popular etymology which compared *Kainulàiset, i.e.* ' Lowlanders,' the name of a Finnish tribe, with an old German word for woman preserved in Engl. *quean, queen.* In later times a race of Amazons was localized in the far north.

Chapter 46.

The Eastern Peoples.

1. Peucinorum: the name is here used as coëxtensive with Bastarnae (see below), a Germanic race of which the Peucini, so-called from Πεύκη, ' Isle of Pines,' their dwelling-place in the delta of the Danube, were strictly only a branch. The hesitancy on the part of Tacitus in classing the Peucini as Teutons is clearly based merely on their proximity to non-Germanic peoples and on the hybrid physical type which resulted from their intermarrying with the Sarmătae. — **Venĕdorum**: they were Slavs — compare the later German designation *Wends* — who lived east of the Vistula, in Poland and adjacent regions.

2. Fennorum: dwelling in Northern and Northeastern Russia. The connection of the name with latter-day Finn, is unmistakable; however, it does not follow from this fact that the ancestors of the enlightened race of modern Finns are to be sought among these peoples to whom Tacitus attributes so low a scale of civilization. — **Sarmatis**: see note on 1. 2. The life here ascribed to them, that of the typical nomads, wandering on horseback or in wagon-houses in quest of pasturage for their herds, is paralleled by the picture given by Herodotus of the Scythians, who once stretched northward from the Danube and the Black Sea. The Scythians had been merged with the Sarmatae as the result of conquest and assimilation.

3. Bastarnas: this brave and warlike people, so early as 200 b.c., had established itself in the lands north of the lower Danube, after an emigration that was first in the historical series of Germanic race movements to the south. Here they were brought into immediate contact with both Greece and Rome, for they served as allies of Philip V of Macedon and of his son Perseus in the Second and Third Macedonian Wars, 200–196

and 171–168 B.C. A century later Mithradates recruited from
them especially efficient forces.

4. sede : *permanence of abode;* they were not nomads as were
the Sarmatae.

5. sordes omnium : a quality attributed in chap. 20. 1 more
particularly to the children. — torpor procerum : said with
reference to times of peace ; recall the general description of the
lethargic existence of the members of the comitatus *quotiens
bella non ineunt,* chap. 15. 1.

6. foedantur : *they show* debasement.

7. ex moribus : *Sarmatarum* is understood.

9. hi . inter Germanos : Tacitus was ignorant of
the basic ethnological distinction between Teuton and
Slav.

10. pedum usu **ac pernicitate** : habitual riders are proverbially
clumsy when on their feet, and besides are generally handicapped
by an apparel or equipment primarily designed for life in the
saddle. Thus, in *Historiae* 1. 79, we read that the Rhoxolani,
a Sarmatian tribe, were quite helpless as foot-soldiers. The Huns
of later history were also inefficient infantrymen, since they were
shod with shapeless boots which impeded their steps (Ammianus
Marcellinus, 31. 2. 6) ; the high-heeled boots of the traditional
American cowboy are ill-adapted to walking.

12. in plaustro : in such folk migrations as that of the Cimbri
and the Teutons, wagons were in daily use among the Germans.
— equo . . . viventibus : the Scythians and the Huns were portrayed as performing on horseback such habitual acts of everyday life as eating, drinking, and sleeping ; cf. Ammianus Marcellinus, 31. 2. 6.

13. foeda paupertas : the level of culture attributed by Tacitus
to the Fenni is practially on a par with that of the famous African
pygmies. — non **arma** : their arrows, employed as a means of
obtaining sustenance, were used only against wild animals, a
state of affairs which coincides with life in the pacific long-ago
approved by Tibullus, 1. 10. 5–6 :

An nihil ille miser (the inventor of " cold steel ") *meruit, nos
ad mala nostra
vertimus in saevas quod dedit ille feras?*

('Or has that unfortunate earned no blame?   Have we turned to our evil purposes what he gave us to use against savage beasts?').

15. asperant: *they tip with.*

16. venatus . . . alit: the pygmies are seldom, if ever, tillers of the soil; they build only temporary habitations as they are always roving from place to place in the forest in pursuit of game.

18. in aliquo ramorum nexu: a wattled shelter of boughs, comparable to the wickiup of the North American Indian.   The dwellings of the pygmies in Africa are arbors constructed of bent, interlaced branches and plantain leaves.

For all Tacitus says to the contrary, these structures of boughs served the Fenni as summer and winter habitations alike; such an arrangement is very improbable in these latitudes and is contradicted by modern conditions among the denizens of these regions.   Among the least civilized branches of Finno-Ugrian races, " the most primitive form of house consists of poles inclined towards one another and covered with skins or sods, so as to form a circular screen round a fire; *winter houses are partly underground.*" *Encyc. Brit.*, 11th ed., vol. 10, p. 392.

20. beatius arbitrantur: Tacitus writes as though their primitive mode of life were the result of deliberate option, whereas, of course, it was due to the fact that they were at a level of culture below those in which agriculture and trade flourish.   The Fenni, it is unnecessary to state, had not indulged in such philosophizing as to the *summum bonum* of existence, but Tacitus, rhetorician and romanticist, poses as the champion of the simple life. — **ingemere:** a figurative expression for hard labor, borrowed from the poets; the editors cite Lucretius, *De Rerum Natura* 5. 209, *vis humana . . valido consueta bidenti ingemere* ('the force of man, accustomed to groan beneath the stout hoe'), and Vergil, *Georgics* 1. 45.   We may add the similar usage in Horace, *Epodes* 5. 29–31, *Veia . . . ligonibus duris humum exhauriebat ingemens laboribus* ('Veia, with the toilsome mattock, was casting up the earth and groaning over her exertions'), though here perhaps the groans were conceived of as literally forthcoming from the toiling witch.

21. inlaborare domibus: the preceding reference to work in the fields, the province of the man, would suggest that we have here, by way of contrast, an allusion to the duties of the home, housework and spinning, regarded as belonging in civilized society to woman's sphere; cf. for example, the famous epitaph of Claudia, Bücheler, *Carmina Epigraphica* 52, *domum servavit, lanam fecit.* Many editors, however, prefer the interpretation *to toil at (building) houses* and assume the allusion to be to the ease with which the shelters referred to above were constructed.

In any case, *inlaborare* is unique in this sense and was perhaps coined by Tacitus to match *ingemere.* — spe metuque : they lived in a "Goldless age, where gold disturbs no dreams" (Byron, *The Island*).

22. versare : *to manipulate* in the activities of trade.

23. rem difficillimam : Tacitus pretends, perhaps somewhat maliciously, that the natural man, here represented by the primitive Fenni, had attained what philosophers of different schools, but especially the Stoics, had exerted themselves through centuries to commend to civilized man as the only source of true happiness, viz. serene indifference to the manifold objects of human desire ; for one exposition of the theme out of many, see Horace, *Epistulae* 1. 6 beginning

> *Nil admirari prope res est una, Numici,*
> *solaque quae possit facere et servare beatum*

(' Indifference to everything is almost the one and only thing that can make and keep one happy, O Numicius '). — ne voto quidem : for the sense compare Horace, *Satires* 2. 6. 1–3 :

> *Hoc erat in votis: modus agri non ita magnus,*
> *hortus ubi et tecto vicinus iugis aquae fons*
> *et paulum silvae super his foret. Auctius atque*
> *di melius fecere.*

(' This was among my prayers : a plot of land of not too great extent, where there would be a garden and, hard by the house, a rill of water ever flowing, and, besides, a bit of woodland. With more generous bounty the gods have favored me ').

24. fabulosa : human credulity in all ages has delighted to people unknown lands with monstrous beings of many kinds. *E.g.* Herodotus, 4. 191, speaks, though skeptically, of the existence in Africa of a 'dogheaded race' and of 'headless men, having their eyes in their breasts'; Othello, Act 1, Scene 3, line 167, woos Desdemona with stories of —

> "The Anthropophagi and men whose heads
> Do grow beneath their shoulders."

On the currency of such tales in 16th century England, see the note on the passage in the *Variorum* edition by Furness. Even the modern world has scarcely ceased to react to reports of the existence of men with monkeys' tails. — **Hellusios et Oxionas**: we can say of these only that they were regarded as denizens of the fabled North.

26. **incompertum**: expressive of an agnostic rather than of a rationalistic, negative attitude.

APPENDIX

Below are tabulated the chief deviations from the text of the *Germania* contained in Halm's fourth edition, which, until the appearance of the second volume of the revision now being prepared by Andresen, must remain the generally accepted means of textual comparison.

B = the Vatican manuscript no. 1862.
b = the Leyden manuscript.
C = the Vatican manuscript no. 1518.
c = the Naples manuscript.
E = the Jesi manuscript.
T = the Toledo manuscript.

CHAPTER		HALM
2. 11.	Ei (BE) . . . **conditoremque** (*conditorisque*, mss.), **Manno**; see Andresen, *Wochenschrift für klassische Philologie*, 1903, col. 276–8; 1910, col. 1317.	et . conditoresque. Manno.
4. 1.	**opinionibus**, mss.	opinioni.
4. 2.	**nullis aliis**.	nullis [aliis].
4. 4.	**tamquam**, B on the margin, Cc; see Andresen, *Jahresberichte des philologischen Vereins zu Berlin*, 28 (1902), p. 308; Zernial, *ibid.* 29 (1903), p. 269 f.	quamquam.
8. 9.	**Veledam**, BcET; *Valedam*, C; *Voledam*, b.	Velaedam.
9. 2.	**Herculem et° Martem**, ET; *Herculem ac Martem*, Cc; *Martem . . . placant et Herculem*, Bb.	Herculem ac Martem.

10. 17.   apud sacerdotes; se enim,
            mss.
11. 3.   pertractentur, BbET.
11. 11.   turbae, mss.
13. 8.   ceteris, mss.
13. 14.   semper et, ET.
14. 12.   enim principis, mss.
16. 10.   lineamenta, BCET.
18. 1–5.   quamquam . . . ambiuntur.
20. 3.   ancillis ac, CcET.
20. 10.   ad patrem, BCcET.
21. 16.   obligantur: victus . . . comis.
            See note on the passage.

25. 1.   descriptis, mss.
26. 3.   in vices, BE.
27. 11   quae nationes, mss.
28. 11.   Germanorum   natione.

30. 1.   ultra hos Chatti initium
            incohant, cE;   *inchoant*,
            CT.
30. 11.   ratione disciplinae, b²c; see
            Müllenhoff, *Deutsche Al-
            tertumskunde*, 4, p. 411;
            r͂oe, CE; r͙e, T; romane,
            B; *romanę*, b.
30. 16.   parare, mss.
31. 14.   vultu, BbET.
35. 2.   redit, mss.
35. 13.   exercitus.
36. 5.   nomina superioris (*nomine
            superioris*, mss.)
37. 18.   consularis, mss.
38. 10.   retro sequuntur, BbET, *se-
            cuntur*, c.

38. 11.	**religatur,** BbET.	religant.
38. 14.	**ut.** See note on the passage.	[ut].
38. 14.	**armantur,** BET in text, all showing a variant *ornantur; ornantur,* b with superscribed *arm; ornantur,* Cc; *armantur,* c², above line.	ornantur.
39. 1.	**vetustissimos se,** BbET.	vetustissimos.
40. 5.	**Nuithones,** BcE.	Nuitones.
41. 6.	**passim et** sine, Cc. See Andresen, *Wochenschrift für klassische Philologie,* 1910, col. 1317; *Jahresberichte des philologischen Vereins zu Berlin,* 36 (1910), p. 281.	passim sine.
. 5.	**peragitur,** mss.	praecingitur.
. 7.	**mansere,** BET.	manserunt.
. 11.	**Lygiorum,** correction in BE.	Lugiorum.
. 13.	**Helisios,** ET; *Helysios,* BCc.	Elisios.
. 27–31.	trans . . . obsequium.	Chapter 44. 1–5.
42. 27.	**Lygios,** BCcET.	Lugios.
43. 4.	**ministrantur,** mss.	ministrant.
45. 3.	**ortus,** CcET.	ortum.
45. 6.	**(et fama vera)**, mss.; editor's parenthesis.	si fama vera.
45. 10.	**omnium,** mss.	omni.
45. 15.	**glesum,** mss.	glaesum.
45. 20.	**profertur,** bET.	perfertur.
45. 22.	**interlucent,** mss.	interiacent (an error).
46. 5.	torpor **procerum,** mss.	torpor: ora procerum.
46. 11.	usu **ac,** mss.	usu et (an error).
46. 14.	**cubile,** mss.	cubili (an error).
46. 15.	**spes,** mss.	opes.

Printed in the United States of America.

CPSIA information can be obtained at www.ICGtesting.com
Printed in the USA
LVOW04s1543181015

458753LV00026B/980/P

9 781330 569672